McCORMICK&SCHMICK'S
SEAFOOD RESTAURANT

Writer and Senior Advisor ▶ William H. P. King

Designer and Project Manager ▶ Judith Ann Rose

Editor ▶ Catherine Gleason

Photographer ▶ Edward Gowans

Food Stylist ▶ Samuel McKean

Word Processing ▶ Foster Productions

Typography ▶ 21st Century Graphics

Printed in Hong Kong
10   9   8   7   6   5

McCormick & Schmick's Management Group
720 SW Washington
Portland, Oregon 97205

International Standard Book Number

    09626697-1-7   Jake's Seafood Cookbook
    09626697-2-5   [hardcover]
    09626697-3-3   McCormick & Schmick's Seafood Cookbook
    09626697-4-1   McCormick & Kuleto's Seafood Cookbook

Library of Congress Catalog Card Number:

    91-75312   Jake's Seafood Cookbook
    91-75310   McCormick & Schmick's Seafood Cookbook
    91-75311   McCormick & Kuleto's Seafood Cookbook

Contents

CHEF TIM HYMES

CHEF DAVID HOLLY

CHEF JOE GONZALES

CHEF WILLIAM KING

CHEF MARCEL LAHSENE

CHEF BILLY HAHN

CHEF CHRIS KEFF

CHEF RENE VANBROEKHUIZEN

CHEF KEN HAYES

CHEF STEVE VICE

CHEF WHITNEY PETERSEN

CHEF JON WIRTIS

Introduction

Imagine a cookbook that was almost twenty years in the making. In a sense, you are holding just such a book. It is the culmination of years of contributions by twelve exceptional chefs, whose collective expertise in seafood cooking is unparalleled. With backgrounds ranging from France to Indonesia to the Northwest, some are graduates of America's finest professional cooking schools, others have honed their skills in our restaurants for their entire careers. They all share important qualities: a love for their work, a respect for tradition, and a dedication to using the freshest and finest ingredients available.

The development of a recipes is a complex challenge. We start with the high standards of quality, freshness, and simplicity originally defined by Bill McCormick in the early 1970's when he re-established Jake's Famous Crawfish Restaurant in Portland, Oregon. Based on the traditions of classic American seafood houses, these standards direct the creative energy of our chefs. Next, our chefs exploit the rich culinary resources of the Northwest and add their own creative touch to each dish. Finally, the recipe is thoroughly tested in our kitchen before it is offered to our guests.

With this book, we have bridged the gap between restaurant dining and home meals by offering professional recipes that are user friendly. From appetizers through soups, salads, pastas, and all types of entrees, we have carefully adapted each recipe for ease of preparation in your home. We have even expressly designed a Fast Fish chapter for your busy household with dinners that can be ready in twenty minutes or less.

This is a book ideally suited for its time. As concerns for health increase, our seafood recipes are a welcome guide to healthier, more delicious eating. Inspired by the culinary focus on restaurant dining and the Pacific Northwest, each recipe is drawn directly from our daily menus. Every chapter is filled with classic fish-house recipes, such as our Dungeness Crab Cakes, Seafood Chowder and Pan-fried Oysters. In addition, we include many contemporary offerings, such as Curried Bay Shrimp and Blueberry Salad, Tuna Tartar, and Mahi Mahi with Mango Orange Barbecue Glaze, to spark your sense of adventure.

In one volume, we bring together the fundamentals of seafood house tradition, diverse Pacific Rim influences and our Northwest heritage, drawn together and refined by the creative efforts of outstanding professional chefs and the discerning tastes of our customers, from whom we have learned so much. We share these gifts with you, that you may share them in turn with your friends and family for many years to come.

Oysters

There are few dining experiences so closely related to the sea as the enjoyment of a freshly opened oyster on the half shell. There are also few other seafoods, or foods of any kind for that matter, so immersed in history and romance.

From the time of the Roman Empire two thousand years ago, man has been captivated by this exalted member of the mollusk family. Much has been written and, in recent years, sophisticated oyster culture has taught us a great deal about proper care and handling.

"'The time has come,' the Walrus said, 'to talk of many things...'"

◄ Oysters on the half shell at Jake's in Portland.

Although Roman legions did collect and transplant oysters near the mouth of the Adriatic Sea before the birth of Christ, it is the Japanese who are generally credited with the development of oyster culture in the early seventeenth century. The Japanese connection proved critical to the Pacific Northwest's oyster industry, which three hundred years later was trying to rebound from disastrous over-harvesting of the indigenous Olympic oyster in the nineteenth century. Attempting to satisfy the enormous demands of Gold Rush era San Francisco, the industry had almost self-destructed.

Willapa Bay, Washington, then known as Shoalwater Bay, had been the repository of a seemingly unlimited supply of the tiny coppery Olympias. They were a staple of the Chinook Indians' diet for centuries, but the insatiable demand for oysters all but rendered the species extinct.

Then along came the Japanese seed or "spat" and oystermen with common sense and a respect for the Northwest's great natural assets. Slowly the process began to reverse. In the last ten or fifteen years, growers with degrees in marine biology and the willingness to experiment with revolutionary oyster culture techniques borrowed from the French established themselves, and oyster cultivation became elevated to state of the art. Now Willapa Bay, along with bays and inlets from Northern California to Southeastern Alaska, produce some of the world's finest oysters. They are truly one of the premier products the region has to offer.

It helps to know your oysters. There's nothing wrong with an "ignorance is bliss" approach to oyster experimentation, but once your passion for them has been established, you'll want to know the subtleties of flavor imparted by each of the different oyster bed locations. Words like coppery, smokey-sweet and cucumber-scented enter the discussion, which sometimes gets a little too intellectual for our taste.

The best way to get to know your oysters is to try them firsthand. Here are a few tips to make your oyster tasting a success.

TYPES OF OYSTERS

There are three basic varieties of oysters grown in the Pacific Northwest: the tiny Olympia, which is no bigger than a quarter and is unique to our region; the European Flat, which is a variation on the French Belon and similar to most East Coast and Gulf of Mexico varieties; and the Pacific, by far the most prominent, which varies in size, shape and flavor, depending upon where it is grown.

Some of the better Pacific oysters come from Shoalwater Bay, Westcott Bay, Quilcene, Hood Canal and Penn Cove, but there are dozens of other growers in British Columbia and along the Northern California, Oregon and Washington coasts producing fine quality oysters.

SIZE

Although each variety is unique in size and shape, generally speaking young oysters, which are smaller, are best for half-shell eating. Olympias range up to 1½"; European Flats, to 4" or 5"; Pacifics, from 2½" to 4" at their longest point.

QUALITY AND FRESHNESS

The quality of an oyster is impossible to tell, until you've looked inside. Ask your fishmonger to open one. If he is reluctant to do so, you're buying your oysters from the wrong person. You want to see lots of liquid inside the shell and plump, clear, bright-looking meat.

If the shell is damaged around its edges or cracked, don't buy it. If the shell is open or gaping even slightly, don't buy it. Any of these characteristics is a sure sign of moisture loss and lack of quality and freshness, as well as poor handling.

Ask for the harvest date of the oysters. (Stores are required to keep these records.) If the oysters have been out of water more than ten days, don't buy them. They may not be spoiled, but quality deteriorates over time.

STORAGE AND HANDLING

If possible, oysters should be positioned with their deepest, cupped side down at all times. This helps ensure moisture retention. When you get them home, scrub them with a brush under cold running water and store them in the coldest part of your refrigerator, covered with a damp cloth. If purchased shortly after they were harvested, they should keep for several days. However, like all seafood, the sooner, the fresher, the better.

OPENING

If you are right-handed, put a kitchen towel in your left hand (if you're left-handed, reverse these directions). Place the oyster on a second, dampened towel on the counter in front of you with the pointed, hinged end pointing to your right. Cover the oyster with your toweled left hand, holding it firmly in place. Insert the point of the oyster knife into the hinge and twist the knife to release the top shell. Slide the knife along the inside of the top shell to separate the connector muscle and remove the top.

Take care not to tip the oyster or you'll lose the liquid we've talked so much about. If there is no liquid and the oyster looks dry and shriveled, discard it. It happens. Even among the best oysters, an occasional one loses its luster.

Slide the knife under the oyster meat to sever the other connector muscle and wipe any loose shell, sand or other debris away with a clean finger.

SERVING

Serve the oysters on a bed of crushed ice. The best way to do this is to place a decoratively folded napkin on a serving plate and put the ice on the napkin. The napkin will absorb what little ice melts. Accompany the oyster with a wedge of lemon and a little mignonette or cocktail sauce. (See recipes, pages 107 & 109.)

Appetizers

First impressions *are* lasting ones. In our business we know that the way in which people are greeted at our door, their initial contact with our service staff and the first food and drink they receive set the stage and create certain expectations.

The appetizer, which is the first course in the progression of a meal, gives you an opportunity to dictate the tone of the evening. Whether it is an elegant dinner party or a casual meal on the patio, your initial presentation will herald what is to follow.

This is where your style can shine. We encourage you to employ your creative energy and have some fun with your preparations. This is also an opportunity to design your entertainment plan with a suitable workload in mind. The last thing you want to do during an evening with guests is to make repeated trips to the kitchen.

The recipes in this section are designed with these factors in mind. Most are "do aheads" with dash!

◄ *Chilled Seafood Appetizer at McCormick & Schmick's in Irvine. Recipe on page 14.*

DUNGENESS CRAB WITH PAPAYA AND AVOCADO

This is a great appetizer to start a very special meal. It's quick and easy, too. The sauce is best made the night before, to allow the flavors to blend.

Serves 4.

1 tablespoon fresh lime juice
⅛ teaspoon saffron
⅔ cup mayonnaise
1 egg yolk
¼ teaspoon ground ginger
1 avocado, firm but ripe
1 papaya, firm but ripe
12 ounces crab meat
Lettuce leaves for underliner, red leaf, green leaf or Bibb

To make the dressing, warm lime juice slightly and add the saffron. Allow the mixture to steep while the juice returns to room temperature. Combine the mayonnaise, egg yolk and ginger and add the lime juice and saffron when it has cooled. Blend well and refrigerate for at least 2 hours, preferably overnight.

When dressing is ready to use, peel, seed and slice the avocado and papaya into 12 slices each. The slices should not be too thick. After slicing, you should have used the entire avocado and ¾ of the papaya.

Pick over the crab meat to make sure there are no bits of shell remaining. Toss the crab meat lightly with 4 tablespoons of the dressing and arrange on lettuce leaves.

Spoon approximately 2 tablespoons of dressing over each plate and complete the arrangement with the sliced avocado and papaya.

Approximate preparation time: 2 hours or overnight for the dressing to rest; 15 minutes to prepare.

TUNA MELT PIZZA

Chef Billy Hahn of the Harborside Restaurant reached back into his childhood for the inspiration for this selection. The Harborside has been offering unique pizzas as part of . menu since opening in 1985. If you make your pizza dough from scratch, we salute you! For those looking for convenience, we offer this rendition on Boboli pizza bread, so readily available in supermarkets today.

Makes 1 pizza, 12" to 14".

4 ounces fresh tuna, cooked, cooled and flaked or chunked
2 tablespoons finely diced onion
1 tablespoon finely diced celery
1 tablespoon finely diced green pepper
1 tablespoon capers
2 tablespoons mayonnaise
1 large Boboli pizza bread
6 ounces mild or medium cheddar cheese, shredded
10 to 12 slices tomato
8 sprigs cilantro
Freshly ground black pepper

Preheat oven to 400°.

Combine the first 6 ingredients. Spread the tuna salad evenly over the surface of the Boboli, leaving a 1" to 1½" border around the edges. Sprinkle cheese over the pizza. Lay tomato slices evenly around. Since you'll be cutting the pizza into 8, each piece should have a tomato slice with the extras arranged in the middle.

Bake for 10 minutes, or until the tomatoes have shriveled a bit and the cheese is brown and bubbly.

Garnish each tomato slice with a leaf of cilantro and grind black pepper over the pizza.

Approximate preparation time: 20 minutes.

Dungeness Crab with Papaya and Avocado ▶

CHILLED EMERALD MUSSELS WITH DIJON MANGO CHUTNEY

Chef Steve Vice serves this dish at Jake's Famous Crawfish Restaurant in Portland using the large, emerald or green lip mussels from New Zealand. However, the dressing works equally well on domestic blue mussels. When blended, the dressing has a creamy texture and the appearance of golden mayonnaise.

Serves 4.

32 emerald mussels
1 cup white wine
3 tablespoons lemon juice
1 tablespoon dijon mustard
1 tablespoon red wine vinegar
¾ cup Major Grey's chutney
Pinch tarragon
⅔ cup olive oil
1 heaping tablespoon finely diced red pepper
1 heaping tablespoon finely diced green pepper
1 heaping tablespoon finely diced red onion
Lemon and parsley to garnish

Scrub the mussels under cold running water and remove the fibrous strands (beards) that may be attached to the shell.

Place the mussels in a saucepan that is just large enough to hold the number of mussels you are to steam.

Add 1 cup of water, the white wine and lemon juice. Cover the pot, bring liquid to a boil and steam the mussels open. Check periodically and remove any mussels as they open. The total cooking time should be 5 to 7 minutes.

Separate the top shell from each mussel and chill the mussels for at least 1 hour.

Meanwhile, prepare the dressing by combining the mustard, vinegar, chutney and tarragon in a food processor or blender until the chunks of chutney have been pureed. Add the oil, a little at a time, with the processor running until the dressing is completely blended.

Transfer the dressing to a mixing bowl and fold in the diced peppers and onion.

Arrange the mussels on serving plates, 8 per person. Spoon about a teaspoon of dressing on each. Garnish with lemon and parsley, and pass additional dressing.

Approximate preparation time: 1 hour to chill; 25 minutes preparation.

PARTY PLATTERS AND SEAFOOD SAMPLERS

Want to feed a crowd without a lot of work and get *oohs* and *aahs* in the process? Present a nice assortment of fresh, cooked and smoked seafood on a large serving tray. Our restaurants offer these platters to the large parties that frequently arrive. At McCormick & Schmick's in Portland we call it "The Big Chill."

Serves 6.

6 ounces dungeness crab meat
6 ounces bay shrimp
12 jumbo prawns, poached and chilled
6 oysters on the half shell
12 whole crawfish, poached and chilled
6 ounces salmon lox
6 ounces smoked sturgeon
Crackers
Dill sauce (See recipe, page 108.)
Cocktail sauce (See recipe, page 109.)
Lemon wedges
Lettuce or curly kale
Sliced tomatoes and red onions
Capers

The procedure is to turn your creativity loose and arrange an attractive display of seafoods and sauces. The tray can be lined with greens, crushed ice, elaborately folded napkins or any combination. Have fun and make it beautiful!

Approximate preparation time: 1 hour.

Chilled Emerald Mussels with Dijon Mango Chutney ▶

SEAFOOD COCKTAILS

Seafood cocktails have been a mainstay of fine restaurant menus since long before any of us can remember, and with good reason. Whether it's crab meat, jumbo prawns or tiny, pink bay shrimp, what can be better than their impeccable freshness and sweet flavors, offset by a lively cocktail sauce.

Serves 2.

6 to 8 ounces fresh dungeness crab meat or
6 to 8 ounces fresh bay shrimp or 12 jumbo prawns,
    peeled and deveined
4 tablespoons cocktail sauce (See recipe, page 109.)
Crushed ice
Lemon wedge
Shredded iceberg lettuce

If you're making prawn cocktails, poach the prawns in water or white wine or a combination of both, flavored with a squeeze of lemon and a pinch of pickling spice. Drain and chill.
    The classic seafood cocktail is served in a pedestal supreme dish designed to hold crushed ice in its base while the seafood sits on top, chilled, but not watered down by the ice. Since most of us don't stock such items in our homes, a nice arrangement can be made by placing a small dish on a nicely folded napkin on a larger plate. Surround the dish with crushed ice, spreading it over the folded napkin. Then put the plates in the freezer until you're ready to serve. At the appointed time, remove the frozen plates. Put some of the shredded lettuce in the dish with a tablespoon of cocktail sauce. Arrange the seafood on top and finish with another spoonful of sauce. Serve a lemon wedge on the side.

Approximate preparation time: 5 to 10 minutes plus 10 minutes to prepare the cocktail sauce.

NOTE: In case you're worried that the ice will melt all over your table, don't. It doesn't take that long to eat a great crab cocktail and the little ice that does melt will be absorbed by the napkin.

◄ *Tuna Tartar*

TUNA TARTAR

This is a contemporary version of the classic beef tartar. If you want to make a dramatic presentation, display the various ingredients separately, then combine them in a large wooden bowl at your table.

Serves 2.

1 hard-boiled egg
6 ounces very fresh loin of tuna, free from sinew
1 tablespoon finely diced red onion
1 tablespoon finely diced green pepper
1 teaspoon capers
1 tablespoon dijon mustard
Red wine vinegar
Olive oil, preferably extra virgin
Salt and freshly ground black pepper
Crackers and/or thinly sliced cocktail rye or black bread

Peel the egg and separate the yolk and white. Chop the yolk and white separately and reserve.
    Thinly slice, then chop the raw tuna with a sharp French knife. This must be done by hand as a food processor or blender will reduce the meat to a pureed texture which is unacceptable. Continue chopping until the tuna is the consistency of coarsely ground beef.
    Arrange the tuna in a mound in the center of a plate and surround it with piles of the diced egg yolk, egg white, red onion, green pepper, capers and dijon.
    Bring the tartar plate to the table along with the oil and vinegar, salt and pepper and a bowl large enough to prepare the mixture.
    Using two dinner forks, combine the tuna with the other ingredients, moisten with oil and vinegar and season with salt and pepper. Serve with fine quality crackers and breads.

Approximate preparation time: 15 minutes, plus 2 to 3 minutes to mix.

CRAB-STUFFED MUSHROOMS

This dish takes us back to the days of "continental" restaurants in the fifties and sixties. A sort of comfort food for chefs, crab-stuffed mushrooms are as good now as they always were and they make a great party hors d'oeuvre as well. Try to select mushrooms that are large: 1½" to 2" in diameter.

Serves 4.

¾ pound crab meat, picked over for shell
½ cup plain bread crumbs
1 celery stalk, minced
1 small onion, minced
1 small green pepper, minced
½ teaspoon dry mustard
¼ teaspoon Tabasco
½ teaspoon lemon juice
¼ teaspoon Worcestershire sauce
¼ cup mayonnaise
1 tablespoon chopped parsley
16 large mushrooms
4 tablespoons grated Parmesan
2 tablespoons melted butter

Preheat oven to 400°.
    Combine all ingredients except the mushrooms, Parmesan and butter. Blend well.
    Rinse the mushrooms and pat dry. Pull the stems out and fill each cavity with about 1 tablespoon of crab mixture. Arrange mushrooms in a baking pan, sprinkle with Parmesan and drizzle with melted butter.
    Bake for 15 minutes, or until nicely browned.

Approximate preparation time: 30 minutes.

BROILED PRAWNS

Prawn is a term used throughout the western United States for the crustacean more accurately called shrimp. No matter what you call them, their versatility and sweetness make for culinary delights. Here are two marinades, used by Chef Ken Hayes at McCormick & Schmick's in Portland, that impart distinctly different yet suprisingly compatible flavors.

Serves 2.

PESTO PRAWNS

8 large prawns (16 to 20 per pound)
3 tablespoons pesto
1 tablespoon olive oil

Peel the prawns, leaving the bottom 1 inch of shell closest to the tail intact. Split the prawns down the back just enough to devein them. Rinse under cold running water.
    Make your favorite pesto recipe or buy a quality commercial pesto and combine with the olive oil. Add the prawns and marinate at room temperature for 1 hour.
    Preheat the broiler, set up the barbecue or set the Jenn-Air grill on high.
    Remove the prawns from the marinade, but don't wipe off the pesto. Cook the prawns for 3 minutes per side, or until they are opaque, basting with the excess pesto.

RASPBERRY PRAWNS

8 large prawns
3 tablespoons raspberry vinegar
2 tablespoons olive oil

Proceed as with the pesto prawns, except that here the marinade is made from raspberry vinegar and olive oil.

Approximate preparation time: 10 minutes preparation; 1 hour to marinate; 6 minutes to cook.

Broiled Pesto Prawns and Raspberry Prawns ▶

BAY SCALLOP SEVICHE

This recipe combines ideas from several of our chefs. Seviche is a very interesting process in which raw seafood is "cooked" by the citric acids of a marinade. Here we use tiny bay scallops, but any mild, lean fish works well.

Serves 4.

1 pound bay scallops
3 limes
3 tablespoons finely diced green pepper
3 tablespoons finely diced red pepper
1 small jalapeño, minced (about 1 teaspoon)
¼ cup finely diced red onion
½ teaspoon cumin
½ teaspoon coriander
Pinch white pepper
1 teaspoon salt
2 tablespoons olive oil
1 tablespoon white wine vinegar
2 tablespoons chopped cilantro
8 small corn tortillas
Oil for frying tortillas

Drain the scallops well and pat dry.
  Combine scallops with the juice from the limes and refrigerate for at least 12 hours. A trick to getting the juice from a lime is to microwave it for 20 seconds first. Make sure the lime juice is not hot when you add it to the scallops.
  Drain off the lime juice. The scallops should look opaque and appear cooked. Combine the scallops with the remaining ingredients (except the tortillas and frying oil). Chill for at least 1 more hour.
  Meanwhile, quarter the tortillas. Heat the oil in a sauté pan and fry the quartered tortillas, a few at a time, for about 1 minute. Sprinkle the cooked chips with salt and serve as an accompaniment to the seviche.

Approximate preparation time: 13 hours to marinate; 20 minutes preparation.

SMOKED TROUT PATÉ

An interesting blend of the smooth richness of cream cheese and the coarse texture of smoked trout, this appetizer is a palate-pleasing prelude to any fine meal. The chefs at McCormick's Fish House in Denver line the molds with plastic wrap for ease in removing the paté. Spraying the molds with non-stick spray also works well.

Serves 4 to 6.

2 tablespoons whole hazelnuts
6 ounces smoked trout (about 1 whole trout)
8 ounces cream cheese
4 ounces butter, very cold or partially frozen
1 teaspoon tarragon
2 teaspoons chives
2 tablespoons brandy
Non-stick spray
2 tablespoons chopped parsley
Crackers or cocktail breads

Preheat oven to 350°.
  Toast the hazelnuts in the oven until lightly browned and beginning to peel. Place the hazelnuts in a brown paper bag to allow their skins to steam a bit. Remove the nuts and rub off the skins. Coarsely chop the hazelnuts and reserve.
  Remove the skin from the trout. Flake it with your fingers or a dinner fork and reserve.
  Soften the cream cheese either by blending it or placing it in the microwave for 30 seconds on high. Dice the butter very small and combine it on the cutting board with the flaked trout. Continue to chop and mix until the butter loses its shape and blends with the trout.
  Combine the trout mixture, cream cheese, tarragon, chives and brandy and blend thoroughly with a wooden spoon. Line 3 ounce or 4 ounce paté molds with plastic wrap or spray them with non-stick spray. Pack the paté into the molds to eliminate air pockets. Chill for at least 2 hours.
  To serve, invert molds on serving plates. Remove molds

(and plastic, if you used that method). Garnish with chopped hazelnuts and chopped parsley, and serve with toasted French bread croutons or fine quality crackers.

Approximate preparation time: 20 minutes preparation; 2 hours to chill.

SEAFOOD MOO SHU

Moo shu sounds exotic, but it's just a quick stir-fry in a wrapper. Dressed up, moo shu is a dazzling appetizer. Dressed down, you have a great snack or light meal. Either way, moo shu is a lot of fun to eat.

Serves 2.

1 tablespoon cooking oil
½ cup rock shrimp, prawns, scallops or any seafood, cut into
    small pieces
½ teaspoon chopped ginger
1 teaspoon chopped garlic
Combine the following for 1½ cups:
    Cabbage, cut into 2" julienne
    Carrots, cut into 2" julienne
    Shiitake mushrooms, cut into 2" julienne
    Zucchini, cut into 2" julienne
1 tablespoon soy sauce
1 tablespoon rice wine vinegar
1 teaspoon sesame oil
1 egg, beaten
4 tablespoons hoisin sauce
2 moo shu wrappers (available in Oriental markets)
Cilantro sprigs for garnish
Chopped green onion for garnish

Heat cooking oil over medium heat. Sauté seafood for 2 minutes. Add ginger, garlic and julienne vegetables and cook for an additional 2 minutes. Add soy sauce, rice wine vinegar and sesame oil and toss. Add beaten egg and cook until egg is firm. Spread hoisin sauce on wrappers. Top with the seafood mixture and garnish with cilantro sprigs and chopped green onion. Fold each wrapper into a cone.

Approximate preparation time: 20 minutes.

Soups & Stews

The recipes in this section run the gambit from the lightest of bisques to the heartiest of meal-in-a-pot stews. There's something for every occasion here. Try the gazpacho as the focal point of a sultry August supper. Start an elaborate meal with the refined lightness of the bisque. Serve the bouillabaisse or cioppino to a crowd, dish out the chowder to your kids.

We use these preparations throughout our menus in a similar manner: for lunches, entrees or first courses. Versatility is the keynote.

◄ *Bouillabaisse as served at McCormick's Fish House in Seattle and Jake's in Portland. Recipe on page 27.*

BAY SHRIMP GAZPACHO

Chilled soups are a great refresher during the heat of the summer. The additions of bay shrimp and homemade tortilla chips add extra interest to the traditional complexity of a classic gazpacho.

Makes 4 bowls or 6 cups.

2 tablespoons chopped garlic
½ cup fresh white bread crumbs, no crusts
3 cups tomato juice
1 green pepper, finely diced (about 1 cup)
4 tomatoes, peeled, seeded and diced (about 3 cups)
½ medium onion, finely diced (about 1 cup)
1 cucumber, peeled, seeded and diced (about 2 cups)
¼ cup olive oil
3 tablespoons red wine vinegar
2 teaspoons salt
1 teaspoon pepper
2 teaspoons cumin
1 teaspoon Tabasco
Oil for frying
8 small corn tortillas, cut into quarters
8 ounces bay shrimp

Combine garlic, bread crumbs, half of the tomato juice, and half of the green pepper, tomatoes, onion and cucumber in a blender or food processor and puree. Combine the puree with the remaining tomato juice, diced vegetables, oil, vinegar and seasonings. Blend with a spoon. Your soup should be very chunky and glossy from the oil.
Heat 1" of oil in a sauté pan and fry tortilla chips for 1 minute, to crisp. Remove and drain on paper towel. Salt lightly.
Garnish each bowl or cup of soup with bay shrimp and tortilla chips.

Approximate preparation time: 45 minutes.

CIOPPINO

Cioppino means seafood soup in Italian, and this dish is said to have evolved from San Francisco fishermen who made use of non-marketable fish in their own soup pots. Evolved it has, into a lusty stew brimming with assorted shellfish. This is the type of dish you need a bib and a bottle of wine to enjoy properly.

Serves 4.

⅓ cup olive oil
2 tablespoons minced garlic
1 small onion, diced
½ pound mushrooms, sliced
1 small green pepper, diced
3 medium tomatoes, peeled, seeded and diced
2 cups crushed tomatoes in puree
1 cup chicken or fish stock
2 cups red wine
2 tablespoons oregano
1 tablespoon black pepper
1 tablespoon salt
¾ pound prawns, peeled and deveined
¾ pound steamer clams, scrubbed and cleaned
¾ pound mussels, cleaned and bearded
1 whole crab, top shell removed, broken into 4 pieces
¾ pound fish filet, bass, rockfish, or cod cut into 8 pieces

Combine olive oil, garlic, onion, mushrooms and green pepper in a large saucepan or stock pot over medium heat. Sauté vegetables until they begin to soften. Add the fresh tomatoes, canned tomatoes in puree, stock, wine and seasonings. Simmer on low heat for 30 minutes. Add the seafood to the pot and simmer for 5 to 10 minutes, or until all the items are cooked.

Approximate preparation time: 1 hour.

Bay Shrimp Gazpacho ▶

NORTHWEST SEAFOOD STEW

Senior Chef Bill King has created a rich stew that evokes its regional origins. It features not only the seafood but also the fabulous hazelnuts and blackberries for which the Pacific Northwest is justly famous.

Serves 4.

¾ cup hazelnuts, toasted and peeled
2 tablespoons margarine
1 tablespoon minced shallots
3 tablespoons flour
1 cup chicken stock or fish stock
1 cup milk
1 cup cream
1 tablespoon butter
1 tablespoon water
½ pound ling cod, true cod or rockfish, cut into
    1½" cubes.
½ pound bay scallops
½ pound shucked yearling oysters
½ pound crab leg or meat picked over for any bits
    of shell
2 tablespoons sherry
2 tablespoons lemon juice
½ cup marionberries or other blackberries, preferably
    fresh, but frozen and thawed are acceptable

Puree toasted, peeled hazelnuts in a blender or food processor. Leave them in the bowl.

Combine margarine and shallots in a large saucepan and sauté over low heat to soften. Add flour to make a roux and continue to cook for 2 to 3 minutes, stirring constantly. Add chicken stock, milk and cream. Bring to a boil, stirring frequently, until thickened.

Pour mixture into the bowl of the blender or food processor and puree with nuts.

Meanwhile, put the butter, water, cod chunks and scallops in the pot and cook over medium heat for 2 minutes. Add oysters and cook for an additional 1 to 2 minutes. Return the pureed mixture to the pot, add crab, sherry and lemon juice and simmer for 2 to 3 minutes.

Puree the berries. Divide soup into 4 bowls and swirl 1 tablespoon of berry puree on top of each as a garnish.

Approximate preparation time: 45 minutes.

SHRIMP BISQUE

This is a light bisque from Chef David Holly of McCormick & Schmick's in San Diego. Unlike many bisques, it isn't heavily laden with cream. Rather it is lightened by the court bouillon in which the prawns are cooked. Use small prawns as they are less expensive and they will eventually be chopped.

Makes 4 cups.

3¼ cups water
2 tablespoons finely diced onion
1 tablespoon finely diced celery
1 tablespoon finely diced carrot
1 teaspoon lemon juice
½ teaspoon white wine vinegar
1 whole clove
1 bay leaf
½ pound prawns, still in their shell
3 tablespoons butter
4 tablespoons flour
¼ teaspoon paprika
⅔ cup milk
⅔ cup cream
1 teaspoon salt
½ teaspoon white pepper
2 tablespoons brandy

Combine the first eight ingredients, bring to a boil, reduce heat and simmer 20 minutes.

Add prawns and simmer 8 minutes, or until fully cooked. Strain liquid and reserve.

When the prawns have cooled slightly, peel, devein and coarsely chop.

Melt butter in a saucepan and add flour and paprika to make a roux. Cook over low heat for 2 to 3 minutes. Add reserved prawn water, stirring constantly. Add milk, cream, salt and pepper. Simmer for 6 to 8 minutes until the bisque has lightly thickened. Add the chopped prawns and brandy and simmer another minute.

Approximate preparation time: 45 minutes.

BOUILLABAISSE

This has always been one of the most popular dishes on the menu at McCormick's Fish House in Seattle. It's a classic and the perfect selection for a crowd or a select few any season of the year. The seafood can be served in its broth or on a platter with the broth passed separately. Either way, make sure you have lots of crusty sourdough bread on hand.

Serves 4.

BROTH
8 cups fish stock (See NOTE.)
1 small onion, diced small
½ green pepper, diced small
3 celery stalks, diced small
2 tablespoons minced garlic
1 tablespoon olive oil
1½ teaspoons cumin
4 teaspoons oregano
1½ teaspoons fennel seed
1½ teaspoons sage
1 bay leaf
1½ teaspoons coriander
4 teaspoons basil
¼ teaspoon cayenne
½ cup white wine
2 cups crushed tomatoes in puree

SEAFOOD
1 whole cooked dungeness crab
8 large prawns
16 steamer clams (about ¾ pound)
16 mussels
1 pound cod, rockfish or other mild fish
8 cooked crawfish

Prepare fish stock. Reserve.

Sauté onion, pepper, celery and garlic in olive oil over medium heat until they begin to soften. Add herbs and spices to the pan and continue cooking for another 2 minutes. Add white wine and tomato and simmer for 5 minutes. Combine stock and vegetable mixture in a large saucepan or stock pot with at least 1 gallon capacity. Simmer for 1 hour.

Meanwhile, prepare the seafood. Discard top shell and break whole crab into 4 pieces. Peel and devein the prawns. Scrub clams and mussels. Cut fish into 2" cubes. Rinse crawfish.

Bring broth to a brisk simmer, but not a full boil. Put crab sections and crawfish in broth for 2 minutes. Add remaining items and simmer. If some ingredients are cooked before the rest, remove them. However, if prepared in this fashion, everything should be done in about 5 minutes.

Remove to individual bowls or serve directly from the pot.

Approximate preparation time: 2 hours.

NOTE: Chicken stock, either homemade or prepared from bouillon cubes, can be substituted if you don't have fish stock.

McCORMICK & SCHMICK'S SEAFOOD CHOWDER

This is one of those signature recipes that contribute greatly to the success of a restaurant over the years. We proudly offer it in publication for the first time ever.

Makes 2 quarts.

2 cups medium diced potatoes, blanched
4 strips sliced bacon, not particularly lean
4 tablespoons margarine
¾ cup flour
¼ cup diced carrot
¼ cup diced onion
¼ cup diced green pepper
¼ cup diced celery
1 quart water
1 8-ounce can clam juice
1½ pounds assorted seafood, cut into ½" cubes and
    poached or sautéed
1½ pounds bay shrimp
1 cup cream
½ teaspoon thyme
¼ teaspoon sage
¼ teaspoon white pepper
¼ teaspoon salt
Butter pats

Blanch the potatoes until just barely tender. Rinse under cold running water, drain and reserve.
    Sauté the bacon in a 4-quart sauce pan over medium heat until it is crisp and all bacon fat has been rendered. Remove the bacon from the pan, dice and reserve.
    Return grease to the pot along with half the margarine. Add flour and cook the roux on low heat for 3 to 4 minutes. Remove roux from pot and reserve.
    Add remaining margarine to pot and sauté carrot, onion, green pepper and celery over low heat to soften.
    Return roux to pot and add the water and clam juice. Raise the heat to high and cook, stirring frequently for 6 to 8 minutes, until thickened. Add seafood, reserved bacon,

potatoes, seasonings and cream. Simmer about 5 minutes.
    Serve in chowder bowls and float a pat of butter on top of each serving.

Approximate preparation time: 40 minutes.

DUNGENESS CRAB AND CORN SOUP

Fresh crab and fresh corn are not always available at the same time of year, but when they are this soup, from McCormick's Fish House in Denver, is at its best. Either ingredient may be used frozen with good results. All or part of this soup may be pureed before the crab is added.

Makes 4 large bowls.

4 cups chicken stock
2 cups corn kernels, freshly cut from the cob, or frozen
¾ cup diced red pepper
½ cup diced green onion
2 tablespoons cornstarch
¼ cup milk
¼ cup cream
1 teaspoon cumin
1 teaspoon salt
1 teaspoon white pepper
½ pound crab meat, picked over for bits of shell

Bring the stock to a boil. Add corn, pepper and onion and simmer 5 minutes.
    Combine cornstarch and milk to form a slurry and add to the stock. Add the cream and seasonings. Return the soup to a boil so the cornstarch thickens the soup.
    At this point you may puree all or part of the soup.
    Divide the crab into four bowls and pour in the soup. The soup will heat the crab meat.

Approximate preparation time: 20 minutes.

◀ *McCormick & Schmick's Seafood Chowder*

Salads

We've come a long way from the wedge of iceberg that so unceremoniously represented this menu category in the fifties and sixties. Today, more license is taken with the creation of salads than with any other element of the meal, making it difficult to define absolutely what is or is not a salad in the first place.

Our approach falls somewhere in between the extremes. We offer salads based on a mixture of greens and some with no greens at all. We prepare pasta salads, but the pasta of choice may be a less traditional, Oriental style. We chill most of our salads, but we also offer salads that are warm and a few that are both. And we exploit the versatility of the genre by presenting salads as appetizers, lunch items and entrees.

All these considerations offer great flexibility, but one rule should be carved in stone: use only the freshest, finest ingredients available. This principle is the foundation of our culinary philosophy.

◄ *Fresh Tuna Niçoise at McCormick & Schmick's in San Diego. Recipe on page 34.*

CURRIED BAY SHRIMP WITH BLUEBERRIES

Fresh blueberries are a must for this recipe. If you use frozen or canned, they will bleed color into the dressing. You can control the spiciness of the dressing by using more or less cayenne pepper. Either way, the blend of flavors improves if you prepare the dressing the night before.

Serves 4.

DRESSING
¼ cup mayonnaise
½ cup plain yogurt
1 tablespoon curry powder
¼ teaspoon cayenne
Pinch salt
1 tablespoon mango chutney (Major Grey's)

SALAD
½ cup chopped green onion (about 8 onions)
2 cups blueberries
2 cups bay shrimp (about 1 pound)
Salad greens
½ medium cantaloupe, peeled and cut into 24 slices

Prepare the dressing by blending the first 6 ingredients. Refrigerate for several hours.
    Chop green onions. Pick over the blueberries to select the nicest ones, reserving a few for garnish. Toss together the onion, berries and bay shrimp and fold in the dressing to blend and coat.
    Tear the salad greens and divide between 4 salad plates, mounding slightly in the middle. Mound the shrimp and berry mixture on each pile of greens.
    Arrange 6 cantaloupe slices as a garnish on each plate along with a few of the reserved blueberries.

Approximate preparation time: 2 to 3 hours to chill and marry the flavors of the dressing; 15 minutes to prepare.

WARM MUSSEL SALAD WITH CITRUS DRESSING

Once obscure and under utilized, mussels are now widely cultivated and popular. This light, flavorful salad is for those who are always looking for a new way to serve mussels.

Serves 4.

4 bunches spinach (enough to make about 8 cups),
    washed and torn
40 to 60 blue mussels (depending on size, about 3 pounds)
¼ cup dry white wine
2 tablespoons lemon juice
6 tablespoons orange juice
1 tablespoon shallots, minced
2 tablespoons finely diced red pepper
2 tablespoons red wine vinegar
¼ cup salad oil
1 teaspoon salt
1 teaspoon ginger
2 hard-boiled eggs, cut into wedges
Orange segments from 2 oranges
4 green onions, sliced

Wash and tear the spinach and mound onto four large salad plates.
    Scrub and debeard the mussels. Place them in a large saucepan with the wine, lemon and orange juices and shallots. Steam mussels over high heat until they open. Remove the mussels and return the liquid to the pot.
    Remove mussel meat from the shells and discard shells.
    Return the mussel meat to the pot along with the red pepper, vinegar, oil, salt and ginger. Heat the mixture on low heat for 1 to 2 minutes.
    Remove the mussel meat and divide between four plates. Pour 3 to 4 tablespoons of the poaching liquid over each salad and garnish with egg wedges, orange segments and green onion.

Approximate preparation time: 30 minutes.

Curried Bay Shrimp with Blueberries ▶

THAI NOODLE SALAD

The kitchen at the Harborside has always had a Southeast Asian influence on its staff. Chef Billy Hahn has used traditional ideas and his own creative skills to produce some terrific dishes with an Asian touch. This salad, which can be served hot or cold, is one of his best and lots of fun to eat.

Makes 2 entree servings or 4 small salads.

DRESSING
¼ cup rice wine vinegar
1 tablespoon minced fresh ginger
¼ cup honey
1 tablespoon soy sauce
1 teaspoon minced fresh garlic
Pinch cayenne
1 tablespoon hot chili oil
1 tablespoon sesame oil
2 tablespoons salad oil

SALAD
5 ounces dry somen noodles, cooked according to
    package directions, drained and rinsed
2 cups fresh vegetables (i.e., carrots, red onion,
    snow peas, celery), julienne cut
6 ounces bay shrimp
8 to 10 soft lettuce leaves, such as butter or red leaf
Sprigs of cilantro

Prepare the dressing by blending all ingredients. Reserve.
    Using two forks or your fingers, combine the cooked noodles, vegetables and bay shrimp.
    Once these are mixed, dress the salad so it is coated thoroughly. The salad is eaten by placing some of the noodle mixture and some cilantro sprigs on a soft lettuce leaf and rolling it up like a soft taco or egg roll.
    If you want to eat the noodles hot, roll them in a hot sauté pan for 1 to 2 minutes. Use the lettuce leaves as an underliner and eat the noodles with a fork or chopsticks.

Approximate preparation time: 30 minutes.

FRESH TUNA NIÇOISE

This is an excellent way to showcase garden-fresh vegetables in the late summer. That is, after all, the origin of this classic from the south of France. Use the best quality fresh tuna to complete this dish and you have a perfect example of the virtues of freshness, quality and simplicity.

Serves 2.

8 ounces fresh, yellowfin tuna steak
5 tiny new red potatoes
15 to 20 young, thin green beans
6 to 8 niçoise or kalamata olives
1 small tomato
½ small red pepper
½ small green pepper
¼ small red onion
1 hard-boiled egg
½ cup vinaigrette dressing made with equal parts extra
    virgin olive oil and balsamic vinegar, flavored with
    fresh basil and garlic
Salt and pepper
Leaf lettuce for underliner

Grill or broil the tuna steak. Allow it to cool, then cut it into large chunks.
    Halve or quarter the potatoes and cook until just tender. Chill.
    Briefly blanch the beans. Rinse under cold water and chill. Cut the vegetables into large chunks or wedges. Quarter the egg.
    Arrange all the elements of the dish on a large serving plate. Splash with some of the vinaigrette and sprinkle with salt and pepper.
    Pass the remaining dressing to dip into as you eat.

Approximate preparation time: 15 to 20 minutes preparation; 20 minutes to chill the tuna, beans and potatoes.

Thai Noodle Salad ▶

HOT SEAFOOD SALAD

Who says salads have to be cold? This version is a recipe inspired by the style of Chef Billy Hahn of the Harborside Restaurant in Portland, that is served with variations in all our restaurants.

Serves 4.

4 bunches spinach (enough to make 8 cups),
    washed and torn.
Combine the following for 3 cups:
    Carrots, 2" julienne cut
    Celery, 2" julienne cut
    Red onion, 2" julienne cut
    Red pepper, 2" julienne cut
¼ cup lemon juice
⅓ cup dry white wine
⅓ cup salad oil
¼ teaspoon salt
¼ teaspoon pepper
¼ teaspoon dill
1 teaspoon minced garlic
1 teaspoon minced shallots
4 ounces bay scallops
4 ounces ling cod, true cod, or rockfish,
    diced into 1" cubes
4 ounces bay shrimp
4 ounces crab meat or crab legs
6 tablespoons grated Parmesan

Mound the spinach on four large salad plates.
    Cut the vegetables into thin, 2" long julienne strips.
    Combine the lemon juice, wine, oil and seasonings in a large sauté pan and bring to a boil. Add garlic, shallots and julienne vegetables and simmer 1 minute.
    Add scallops and fish and simmer 1 minute. Add shrimp and crab. Simmer 1 final minute.
    Arrange the seafood on the spinach and pour the liquid over each as a dressing. Sprinkle with Parmesan.

Approximate preparation time: 20 minutes.

SPICY NOODLE AND BAY SHRIMP SALAD

This dish has been on the permanent printed menu of Jake's Famous Crawfish Restaurant in Portland for quite sometime. It's a real favorite with our lunch crowd. You can control the "heat" in the dressing by varying the amount of cayenne you use.

Serves 4.

DRESSING
¾ cup smooth peanut butter, or crunchy if you like
    more texture
1 cup chicken stock, chilled, homemade or made from
    instant bouillon cubes
5 tablespoons orange juice
2 tablespoons rice wine vinegar
1 tablespoon crushed red pepper flakes
Large pinch cayenne pepper

SALAD
8 ounces dried pasta, oriental udon or linguini noodles
8 ounces bay shrimp (about 2 cups)
Combine the following for 1½ cups:
    Celery, cut into 2" julienne
    Carrot, cut into 2" julienne
    Red onion, cut into 2" julienne
Lettuce leaves, for underliner
½ red pepper, cut julienne for garnish
Cilantro, for garnish

Combine the first 6 ingredients and blend well. Reserve.
    Cook the noodles according to package directions.
Rinse under cold water, drain and reserve.
    Prepare the vegetables.
    Arrange lettuce leaves on four plates. Toss noodles with the dressing and mound on lettuce leaves. Scatter the julienne vegetables on the noodles. Top with bay shrimp and garnish with red pepper and sprigs of cilantro.

Approximate preparation time: 20 minutes.

LEMON PEPPER PRAWN SALAD

This is one of the first recipes Chef Rene VanBroekhuizen created for McCormick & Kuleto's Restaurant in San Francisco, California. It has been a favorite ever since.

Serves 4.

DRESSING
¾ cup lemon juice
1 cup olive oil
½ teaspoon salt
½ teaspoon coarsely ground black pepper
½ teaspoon thyme, fresh if possible
2 teaspoons sugar

SALAD
16 jumbo prawns, peeled and deveined
6 radishes, julienne cut
¼ red onion, cut into 1½" julienne
1 carrot, cut into 1½" julienne
½ cucumber, cut into 1½" julienne
6 cups salad greens, washed and torn
2 tomatoes, cut into 8 wedges each
4 hard-boiled eggs, quartered

Preheat broiler or range-top grill.
   Combine the first 6 ingredients and blend well. Divide the dressing into 2 equal amounts. Set one aside. Marinate the prawns in the remaining dressing.
   While the prawns are marinating, prepare the radishes, onion, carrot, onion, cucumber and greens and combine. Wedge cut the tomatoes, quarter the eggs and set aside.
   Drain prawns and discard marinade. Broil the prawns for 2 to 3 minutes on each side, until opaque throughout.
   Toss the greens mixture with the reserved dressing and arrange on dinner plates. Top with 4 prawns each.
   Garnish with the quartered egg and tomato wedges.

Approximate preparation time: 20 minutes to prepare; 30 minutes to marinate.

BAY SHRIMP AND SPINACH WITH WARM BACON DRESSING

This salad makes a great lunch or light supper. The dressing is one that has been used extensively in our restaurants for years. Made in advance, it can be refrigerated and reheated as needed. Remember, this is a warm dressing, not hot. The idea is that the dressing wilts the spinach slightly and serves as a nice counterpoint to the chilled shrimp.

Serves 4. Makes about 2 cups of dressing.

DRESSING
1 pound bacon, diced very fine
1 tablespoon dried basil
1½ teaspoons marjoram
1 teaspoon salt
½ teaspoon pepper
1 cup red wine vinegar
1 tablespoon lemon juice
¼ teaspoon finely chopped garlic
⅓ cup sugar

SALAD
2 bunches fresh spinach
1 pound bay shrimp
4 hard-boiled eggs, coarsely chopped
20 black olives
1 tomato, cut into 8 wedges
⅔ cup dressing
4 tablespoons freshly grated Parmesan

Prepare the dressing by frying or baking the bacon. Whichever way you cook it, do so at medium heat. The object is to brown and crisp the bacon bits while rendering as much fat as possible. Whatever you do, don't allow the bacon to burn. You should end up with approximately ¾ cup of rendered bacon grease.
   While the bacon is cooking, combine the remaining dressing ingredients.

When the bacon is well browned, pour off the grease into a heat-proof measuring cup. Combine the cooked bacon and ¾ cup bacon grease with the already mixed ingredients. Blend thoroughly. Reserve ⅔ cup and warm on low heat. (The remaining dressing should be refrigerated.)

Clean the spinach, removing the heavy stem portions of the leaves. Tear the spinach into bite-size pieces.

Have all the remaining ingredients ready so the salad comes together quickly once the spinach is tossed. Toss the spinach with the dressing and arrange on four salad plates. Top each with a mound of bay shrimp. Sprinkle with chopped egg, arrange olives and tomato and finish with a sprinkle of Parmesan cheese.

Approximate preparation time: 40 minutes.

BLACKENED SALMON SALAD

During the cajun craze, our restaurants developed many recipes based on the blackening technique of Chef Paul Prudhomme. This dish, from McCormick's Fish House in Seattle, is a combination of vivid flavors and an example of the contrast between hot and cold that can provide great culinary interest.

Serves 4.

DRESSING
1 cup finely chopped green onions
2 tablespoons whole grain mustard
Pinch tarragon
2 egg yolks
¼ teaspoon salt
¼ teaspoon pepper
1 tablespoon white wine vinegar
½ cup mayonnaise, homemade or commercial

SALAD
1 pound boneless salmon filet, cut into 20 fingers, 2" long
Salad oil or non-stick spray
4 tablespoons cajun magic or homemade cajun spice
 (See recipe, page 109.)
Salad greens, about 1½ cups per salad
4 hard-boiled eggs, quartered
4 artichoke hearts, cut in half
1 tomato, cut into 8 wedges
16 black olives

Prepare the dressing by placing the chopped green onions in the bowl of a food processor or blender and chop further. The onions should be like coarsely chopped parsley. Add the next 7 ingredients and blend thoroughly.

Brush salmon fingers lightly with oil or spray with non-stick vegetable oil spray, then coat with cajun spice.

Heat a sauté pan over medium-high heat. When the pan is hot, add salmon and cook on one side for 2 minutes, or until well browned. Turn and continue cooking for another 1 to 2 minutes. The salmon should be darkly browned (but not black) on the outside and pink and just barely cooked through on the inside.

Toss the greens with ⅓ of the dressing and arrange them to cover half of each of five salad plates. Spread the remaining dressing over the exposed half of each plate and place four fingers of salmon on each pool of sauce.

Garnish the salads with egg and tomato wedges, artichoke hearts and olives.

Approximate preparation time: 30 minutes.

NOTE: True blackening requires a very hot cast-iron skillet and an extremely powerful exhaust fan. We don't consider it a safe process to perform at home, so this is a less extreme "bronzing" technique.

Fast Fish

You just arrived home from your third, straight ten-hour day. Your spouse has a meeting at 7:30. One of the children needs a ride to baseball practice and the other one has a date. Who are you going to call? Well, it's probably home delivery pizza and who would blame you! But just in case you choose to steadfastly maintain your commitment to a quality meal, here are a handful of recipes to save the day.

In selecting dishes for this section, our dilemma was what *not* to choose. Most of our recipes come together relatively quickly, with good reason. Our restaurants are very busy places, almost as busy as your home. So most of our preparations are designed for quick cooking times. The straightforwardness of our style is also conducive to this approach. We hope it serves you well in times of need and on those more relaxed days when you want a delicious meal with a minimum of fuss.

Steamed Clams at McCormick's Fish House in Denver.
◀ *Recipe on page 48.*

GRILLED TUNA WITH CITRUS SHALLOT VINAIGRETTE

This is a balanced sauce that works well with the assertive flavor of tuna. We've also served it with salmon, where it's a nice foil to the richness of the fish.

Serves 2.

1 lemon, zest and juice
1 lime, zest and juice
1 tablespoon rice wine vinegar
2 tablespoons shallots, sliced into rings
1 tablespoon sugar
1 tablespoon oil
¼ teaspoon crushed red pepper
Oil or non-stick spray
2 yellowfin tuna steaks, 6 to 9 ounces each and at least
    1" thick

Preheat the grill.
    Using a swiveled-edge vegetable peeler, remove the outside peel of the lemon and lime. Try not to take the white pith along with the peel. Julienne the peel.
    Bring a cup of water to boil and drop the julienne peel in for 30 seconds. Drain into a strainer and rinse with cold water. Squeeze the juice from the lemon and lime and combine with the peel, vinegar, shallots, sugar, oil and crushed red pepper to create the vinaigrette.
    Coat the tuna steaks lightly with oil or spray with non-stick spray. Grill for 2 to 3 minutes per side, basting with a little of the liquid from the vinaigrette.
    Remove to plates and top with remaining vinaigrette.

Approximate preparation time: 15 minutes.

PAN-FRIED OYSTERS

This is a traditional fish house recipe and one that is a specialty in all our restaurants. The trick is in the technique: the right pan, the right amount of oil heated to the right temperature and a very brief cooking time. Shucked oysters are packaged according to size. Yearlings are not only the smallest—about 20 to 25 per pint—they are the best!

Serves 2.

1 pint shucked yearling oysters
⅓ cup flour
1 teaspoon salt
1 teaspoon flour
¼ cup oil, for frying
Lemon wedge
¼ cup tartar sauce (See recipe, page 107.)

Season the flour with salt and pepper and coat the oysters well, shaking off the excess.
    Heat the oil in a 10" to 12" sauté pan. If the pan is any smaller, the oil will be too deep and the oysters won't panfry. If the pan is too big, the oil will spread too much and the oysters will burn. Heat the oil until it just begins to smoke. If the oil is too hot, the oysters will burn. If not hot enough, the oysters will be soggy and lack crispness.
    Slip the floured oysters into the hot oil and shake a little to keep them separate. Panfry the oysters for 1 minute, turn and fry for 30 seconds on the other side. The oysters should be crisp and golden brown on both sides.
    Remove the oysters with a slotted spoon or spatula and drain on paper towels.
    Serve the oysters with lemon and tartar sauce.

Approximate preparation time: 10 minutes.

◀ *Grilled Tuna with Citrus Shallot Vinaigrette*

GRILLED PRAWNS WITH TOMATO AND GREEN PEPPERCORN SAUCE

The prawns in this dish can be prepared in several ways. At McCormick's Fish House in Denver, they are dusted in flour, then grilled in butter on the griddle. At home, you can sauté them or, if you have a Jenn-Air or other range-top system, skew them on bamboo sticks and grill them as brochettes. In the summer, the barbecue grill is the ideal place to prepare these delicious prawns.

Serves 4.

½ cup peeled, seeded and diced tomatoes
3 tablespoons butter
1 tablespoon green peppercorns
½ cup white wine
1 tablespoon chopped shallots
1 tablespoon chopped parsley
24 jumbo prawns, peeled and deveined

Reduce the wine over high heat until you have ¼ cup, cool to room temperature.
    Combine the cooled wine with the remaining ingredients except the prawns and reserve.
    Broil or grill the prawns, taking care not to overcook them. They should be pink and opaque but not dry or tough.
    Arrange prawns, 6 to a portion, on dinner plates and pour sauce evenly over them.

Approximate preparation time: 20 minutes.

MIXED SEAFOOD SALAD

Leftovers can be a luxury if you have a good way to use them. Here's a recipe that makes a great lunch or quick light dinner from leftover fish. Any combination of cooked seafood works. This one uses bay shrimp, crab meat and flaked salmon.

Serves 4.

8 cups salad greens, washed and torn
1½ cups 1000 Island Dressing (See recipe, page 108.)
8 ounces crab meat
8 ounces bay shrimp
8 ounces cooked salmon, flaked
16 black olives
4 hard-boiled eggs, quartered
1 tomato, cut into 8 wedges

Toss the greens with ½ the dressing and mound on 4 large plates. Arrange the seafood in three strips or mounds on the lettuce and garnish with the olives, eggs and tomato.
    Serve the remaining dressing on the side, to accompany the seafood.

Approximate preparation time: 10 minutes.

Grilled Prawns with Tomato and Green Peppercorn ▶
Sauce

BAY SHRIMP QUESADILLAS

Here's a great recipe for a busy family. It's quick, easy, versatile, and kids love it. Serve these quesadillas as the beginning of a Southwestern seafood meal or use them for lunch or snacks. If you have a Jenn-Air or other range-top system, the pancake griddle attachment makes these a breeze.

Makes 4 small quesadillas.

2 cups shredded jalapeño jack cheese (or cheddar
    cheese for a mild version)
1 cup bay shrimp, about ½ pound
¼ teaspoon cumin
8 small tortillas
4 tablespoons butter
1 cup salsa (See recipe, page 108.)

Combine the shredded cheese with the bay shrimp and cumin.
    Lay out 4 of the tortillas and divide the mixture evenly between them. Top with 4 remaining tortillas.
    Melt the butter on the griddle or in sauté pans and brown the quesadillas over low to medium heat, 2 to 3 minutes per side. Remove to a cutting board and allow the melted cheese to "set" for a minute. Otherwise, when you cut the quesadillas, you will lose half the cheese on the board.
    Quarter the quesadillas and serve with salsa.

Approximate preparation time: 15 minutes, plus 15 minutes if you wish to prepare fresh salsa.

ROCK SHRIMP DIJON

Here's a delicious, quick recipe. Once you've pulled all the ingredients together, dinner is ready in less than 5 minutes. The dijon and basil complement each other beautifully.

Serves 2.

1 tablespoon butter
2 green onions, sliced (about 3 tablespoons)
8 to 10 medium mushrooms, quartered (about 1 cup)
½ pound rock shrimp
2 teaspoons chopped shallots
2 teaspoons chopped garlic
2 tablespoons lemon juice
½ cup cream
2 tablespoons shredded fresh basil
2 tablespoons dijon mustard

Melt butter over high heat. Add the onions and mushrooms. Sauté for 1 minute. Add rock shrimp, shallots and garlic. Sauté for 1 minute. Add remaining ingredients and bring to a boil to reduce. Finish cooking for 1 more minute.
    If your sauce is not thick enough to coat a spoon, remove the shrimp and mushrooms to a serving plate and cook sauce for 1 final minute before pouring over the shrimp.

Approximate preparation time: 15 minutes.

RED ROCKFISH WITH ROASTED RED PEPPER BUTTER

Compound butters, such as this roasted pepper butter, can turn a simple piece of baked, broiled or poached fish into something special. The fish itself is your choice—orange roughy, rockfish, cod, sea bass, etc., or a mixed grill showcasing several fish.

Serves 4.

4 portions rockfish, 6 to 8 ounces each
Oil or non-stick spray
4 tablespoons roasted red pepper butter
    (See recipe, page 107.)

Preheat broiler or grill.
    Lightly coat the fish with oil or non-stick spray and grill for 2 minutes on each side over high heat for thin filets, or 3 to 4 minutes for thicker varieties, until opaque and just cooked through.
    Place filet on dinner plates. Place medallions or rosettes of the butter on the filets and serve immediately.

Approximate preparation time: 10 minutes.

NOTE: Compound butters can be prepared in advance and kept in your freezer.

STEAMED CLAMS

The tiny butter clams indigenous to the Pacific Northwest are ideal for steaming. The variety called Manila are best. Steamers are a nice start to a meal or a meal in themselves. This recipe can be extended to serve a couple or a crowd.

Serves 2.

2 pound clams
4 tablespoons sherry
4 tablespoons dry white wine
½ teaspoon minced shallots
½ teaspoon minced garlic
½ teaspoon lemon juice
6 tablespoons drawn butter

Choose the right size saucepan or stock pot for the amount of clams you are preparing. You will need about 1 quart of capacity per pound of clams.
    The rest is easy. Combine all ingredients in the pot over high heat. Cover and allow the clams to steam until they open. Depending on the type, size and age of the clams, this will take 3 to 8 minutes. Remove the clams to a serving bowl and return the broth to the pot. Simmer to reduce for 1 or 2 minutes.
    Serve the broth and the drawn butter in separate ramekins along with the clams and pass the crusty French bread.

Approximate preparation time: 10 minutes.

OYSTER STEW

If there was ever a culinary example of the old adage less is more, this is it. From the old seafood houses of New England and San Francisco to our tables today, the perfect oyster stew is perfectly simple.

Serves 2.

1 pint heavy cream (or milk, if you prefer your stew
    a bit lighter)
24 shucked yearling oysters
Pinch salt
Pinch white pepper
1 tablespoon butter
2 teaspoons chopped parsley
Oyster crackers

Heat the cream in a sauté or saucepan to a simmer. Do not let it boil. Add the oysters and simmer until the edges of the oysters curl. This only takes 1 or 2 minutes. Season with salt and pepper.
    Transfer the stew to two serving bowls, dividing the oysters evenly. Cut the butter into 2 pats and float on the top of each stew. Sprinkle with a little chopped parsley.
    Serve with oyster crackers.

Approximate preparation time: 5 minutes.

GRILLED DUNGENESS CRAB AND BAY SHRIMP SANDWICH

We're always looking for sandwich ideas to add to our menus. Whether you are eating in one of our restaurants in Seattle, Portland, San Francisco, Southern California or Denver, you're likely to run across this one. It's an elegant way to dress up an old standard. The tomatoes, dipped into a good vinaigrette dressing, add further interest and flavor.

Serves 2.

6 slices ripe red tomato
3 tablespoons vinaigrette dressing (See NOTE.)
4 slices firm textured wheat or sourdough bread
4 slices cheese, havarti, jack or cheddar
4 ounces crab meat
4 ounces bay shrimp
Butter or margarine for grilling

Preheat the stove top griddle or sauté pan on medium.
    Coat the tomato slices with the vinaigrette and construct sandwich with the cheese on either side of the crab, shrimp and tomato. Grill until the cheese has melted and the bread is nicely browned.

Approximate preparation time: 10 minutes.

NOTE: Make 1 cup vinaigrette dressing with ½ cup each virgin olive oil and balsamic vinegar, 1 tablespoon chopped fresh basil leaf, 1 teaspoon finely minced garlic and a pinch each of salt and pepper.

Pasta

Trends in the American culinary scene come and go as frequently as their counterparts in the world of fashion. The annual publication of so called "What's Hot & What's Not" lists can keep anyone trying to keep pace running from specialty grocery to cookbook store and back. But pasta seems to have been elevated to a level above the fray. That's fine with us. We love pasta and consider it an important component of our restaurants' menus.

Like everything in the food world, the move in pastas is toward lighter preparations. So much the better! They are healthier, faster and easier to prepare. No hours of simmering and stirring. They are an excellent option in a busy, health-conscious country.

But with all the talk (and genuine concern) about lighter, healthier alternatives, guess which pastas are most popular with our customers? Discretion being the better part of valor, we'll let you draw your own conclusions from a wide variety of pasta styles.

◄ *Linguini with Tomato Basil Saffron Broth and Shellfish at McCormick & Schmick's in Portland. Recipe on page 52.*

LINGUINI WITH TOMATO BASIL SAFFRON BROTH AND SHELLFISH

We like to offer pastas that are light without a lot of cream, butter or heavy sauces. Here is one designed by Senior Chef Bill King that's full of flavor and chock full of shellfish. Fresh basil is best, but dried will work in a pinch.

Serves 4.

1 pound linguini noodles
1 large tomato, diced
1 cup tomato puree
2 cups chicken stock or fish stock
½ cup olive oil
4 tablespoons minced garlic
1 cup shredded fresh basil or 2 tablespoons dried basil
1 teaspoon saffron steeped in ¼ cup hot water
1 teaspoon fresh ground black pepper
12 mussels (about ½ pound)
12 clams (about ½ pound)
12 jumbo prawns, peeled and deveined
½ pound bay scallops
½ pound crab legs
Grated Parmesan

Cook pasta al dente, rinse in cold water, drain and reserve. Return a pot of water to the stove, put a colander in it and bring water to a boil.

Combine tomato, tomato puree, stock, oil and seasonings in a large saucepan and bring to a boil. Simmer for 5 minutes. Add shellfish in the following order, letting each ingredient cook 1 minute before adding the next: mussels and clams, prawns, scallops, and crab legs.

Meanwhile, put cooked pasta in colander in boiling water for 1 minute, drain and add it to the seafood. Toss to coat.

Serve this in large soup or pasta bowls with the pasta mounded in the middle. Surround with shellfish and broth. Sprinkle with Parmesan.

Approximate preparation time: 20 minutes.

TORTELLONI WITH CRAB AND GORGONZOLA

Senior Chef Marcel Lahsene of Jake's Famous Crawfish Restaurant in Portland created this recipe out of his love for the sharp gorgonzola that flavors the sauce. As with most of our pasta recipes, it's best if you precook the tortelloni, then roll them into the sauce when you are ready to serve. This technique gives you more control over the overall dish as you are able to concentrate on the seafood and sauce at service time.

Serves 2.

½ pound dry or 1 pound fresh tortelloni, cheese filled, precooked, rinsed and drained
6 ounces dungeness crab meat
6 ounces gorgonzola cheese
2 tablespoons butter
2 teaspoons minced shallots
¼ cup dry white wine
½ cup cream
Salt and pepper to taste
1 tablespoon chopped parsley

Pick over the crab meat to remove any lingering shell fragments. Set aside ⅓ of the crab for a garnish.

Crumble the cheese.

Sauté the shallots in butter over low heat until softened. Add wine and cream and heat to a boil. Add crumbled cheese and ⅔ of the crab. Reduce the sauce over high heat for 1 minute. Add the tortelloni and continue cooking over high heat for another 2 minutes.

Season with salt and pepper and remove to dinner plates.

Garnish the tortelloni with reserved crab and sprinkle with chopped parsley.

Approximate preparation time: 20 minutes.

Tortelloni with Crab and Gorgonzola ▶

ROCK SHRIMP RADIATORE

This sauce works well with oddly shaped pastas like radiatore, fusilli or casariccia. Their sturdy texture holds up well to the rich dijon cream treatment.

Serves 2.

6 ounces dry or 1 pound fresh pasta
2 tablespoons butter
1 cup sliced mushrooms
8 ounces rock shrimp
½ cup tomato, peeled, seeded and diced
2 tablespoons dijon mustard
¾ cup cream
½ cup grated Parmesan
1 tablespoon fresh basil, shredded

Cook pasta al dente, rinse in cold water, drain and reserve. Return a pot of water to the stove, put a colander in it and bring water to a boil.

Melt the butter over medium heat and sauté mushrooms for 1 or 2 minutes, until they begin to soften. Add rock shrimp and continue to sauté for 2 minutes. Add tomatoes, mustard, cream, Parmesan and basil and simmer for 2 to 3 minutes.

Dip the pasta in boiling water, drain and add to the shrimp and sauce. Toss to combine and coat.

Approximate preparation time: 15 minutes.

FETTUCINI AND PRAWNS WITH POPPY SEEDS AND LEMON

This is a very light and clean-tasting pasta dish that doesn't rely on heavy sauces or on a surplus of ingredients. Delicate is the keynote here. It's a refreshing variation.

Serves 4.

1½ pounds fresh fettucini noodles
¼ pound butter
1 teaspoon minced garlic
2 teaspoons minced shallots
24 jumbo prawns, peeled and deveined (about 1¼ pounds)
2 tablespoons lemon juice
½ cup chopped green onion
¾ cup chicken stock
2½ tablespoons poppy seeds
½ teaspoon salt
½ teaspoon pepper

Cook pasta al dente, rinse in cold water, drain and reserve. Return a pot of water to the stove, put a colander in it and bring water to a boil.

Meanwhile, sauté the garlic, shallots and prawns over medium heat, in the butter. Turn the prawns after 2 minutes and add lemon juice, green onion, chicken stock, poppy seeds, salt and pepper. Reduce to a simmer.

Drop the cooked pasta in the boiling water for 1 minute. Remove the colander, drain the pasta and add it to the prawns and sauce.

Toss to coat thoroughly and divide between four plates.

Approximate preparation time: 15 minutes.

Rock Shrimp Radiatore ▶

OYSTERS and ANGEL HAIR

One of the most important considerations when pairing a specific pasta shape or size with the other ingredients in a dish is, do they match? In this case, delicate oysters are paired with the most delicate of pastas—angel hair—along with a rich but light cream sauce.

Serves 4.

1½ pounds fresh angel hair pasta
1 cup cream
1 cup milk
1⅓ cups dry white wine
1 tablespoon minced garlic
4 tablespoons minced shallots
2 pints shucked yearling oysters (40 to 50 oysters)
1 teaspoon salt
1 teaspoon white pepper

Cook pasta al dente, rinse in cold water, drain and reserve. Return a pot of water to the stove, put a colander in it and bring water to a boil.
   Combine cream, milk, wine, garlic and shallots in a large sauté pan or pot and bring to a boil. Simmer for 2 to 3 minutes. Add the oysters, salt and pepper and continue cooking for 2 to 3 minutes. When the oysters curl around the edges, they are done. Add the pasta and toss to coat and heat thoroughly.

NOTE: This is a light sauce with no thickening outside the residual starch from the pasta. The light consistency of this dish requires you serve it in bowls rather than on plates.

Approximate preparation time: 15 minutes.

SCALLOP and BAY SHRIMP FETTUCINI with PARMESAN CREAM

This is the all-time favorite pasta dish prepared at McCormick & Schmick's in Portland. Even with the trend toward lighter pasta sauces, diners return again and again for a bowl of this creamy creation.

Serves 2.

½ pound dry or ¾ pounds fresh fettucini
2 tablespoons butter
4 teaspoons minced garlic
2 teaspoons minced shallots
1⅓ cups cream
1 cup fresh, grated Parmesan
4 ounces bay scallops, about ½ cup
4 ounces bay shrimp, about ½ cup
1 tablespoon chopped parsley

Cook pasta al dente, rinse in cold water, drain and reserve.
   Melt butter in a large sauté pan over medium heat. Add garlic and shallots and cook until softened.
   Add cream and Parmesan and cook over high heat for 1 minute to reduce. Add scallops and continue to cook 1 more minute. Add pasta and bay shrimp and toss to blend. Cook for an additional 1 to 2 minutes to heat thoroughly.
   Divide between 2 plates, sprinkle with parsley and pass extra Parmesan at the table.

Approximate preparation time: 15 minutes.

SALMON LINGUINI WITH SOUR CREAM AND DILL

From McCormick's Fish House in Seattle comes this fabulous recipe for leftover or extra salmon. The flavors of the dill and capers are rather sharp and create an interesting combination with the pasta and cream.

Serves 2.

½ pound dry or ¾ pound fresh fettucini
2 tablespoons butter
8 ounces salmon, cut into 1" cubes
2 tablespoons white wine
½ cup cream
1 cup sour cream
¼ teaspoon salt
¼ teaspoon white pepper
2 tablespoons chopped fresh dill (or 2 teaspoons dry dill)
Dash Worcestershire sauce
2 tablespoons capers
½ teaspoon lemon juice

Cook pasta al dente, rinse in cold water, drain and reserve. Return a pot of water to the stove, put a colander in it and bring water to a boil.

Melt butter over medium heat and sauté the salmon chunks for 1 minute. Add wine for 30 seconds to deglaze pan. Add remaining ingredients and simmer for 3 to 4 minutes.

Dip pasta in colander in boiling water for 1 minute and then drain and add to the salmon and sauce, tossing to blend and coat.

Approximate preparation time: 15 minutes.

FETTUCINI WITH ROCK SHRIMP, BASIL AND SUN-DRIED TOMATOES

This dish takes advantage of the natural affinity that basil and sun-dried tomatoes have for each other. Add some rock shrimp, garlic and Parmesan and you have a pasta dish full of lively flavors.

Serves 2.

½ pound dry or ¾ pound fresh fettucini
2 tablespoons butter
1 cup sliced mushrooms
8 ounces rock shrimp
2 tablespoons sun-dried tomatoes, julienne cut
1 tablespoon minced garlic
2 tablespoons basil leaves, julienne cut
1 tablespoon minced green onion
¼ cup chicken stock
¾ cup cream
½ cup grated Parmesan

Cook pasta al dente, rinse in cold water, drain and reserve. Return a pot of water to the stove, put a colander in it and bring water to a boil.

Melt butter over medium heat and sauté mushrooms for 2 to 3 minutes, until they brown and soften. Add rock shrimp, sun-dried tomatoes and garlic and continue cooking for another 2 minutes. Add remaining ingredients and simmer for 2 minutes.

Dip pasta in boiling water for 1 minute, drain and add to the pan with the rock shrimp and sauce.

Approximate preparation time: 15 minutes.

FISHERMAN'S FETTUCINI

Here's a meal that can come together in minutes, particularly if you use a good quality commercial chunky pasta sauce to produce it. The selection of seafood depends on your preference and the contents of your refrigerator— just as this dish was dictated by the day's extra catch for the coastal fishermen who inspired it.

Serves 4.

1 pound dry or 1½ pounds fresh fettucini noodles
½ cup white wine
2 tablespoons garlic, minced
3 cups chunky pasta sauce, homemade or commercial
1 dozen clams
1 dozen mussels
8 ounces fish filet (such as roughy, cod, rockfish, snapper or bass)
½ pound scallops
Parmesan cheese

Cook pasta al dente, rinse in cold water, drain and reserve. Return a pot of water to the stove, put a colander in it and bring water to a boil.
    Place wine and garlic in a large sauté or saucepan big enough to hold seafood and sauce. Bring to a boil and add seafood.
    Dip colander of pasta in water for 2 minutes to heat.
    When seafood has cooked and the wine is almost evaporated, approximately 3 minutes, add tomato sauce and toss to heat thoroughly.
    Remove pasta from water and drain. Divide between 4 pasta bowls and top with seafood and sauce, making sure you give even amounts to everyone. Pass the Parmesan!

Approximate preparation time: 15 minutes.

GARLIC, PRAWN AND OYSTER FETTUCINI

This aggressively seasoned pasta is a bestseller at McCormick's Fish House in Denver. It is another example of a dish that comes together in minutes, yet has a complexity of flavors that suggests hours in the kitchen.

Serves 4.

1 pound dry or 1½ pounds fresh fettucini noodles
12 jumbo prawns, peeled and deveined (about ¾ pound)
¼ pound butter
2 cups chicken stock
¼ cup garlic, minced
4 teaspoons cajun magic or homemade cajun spice (See recipe, page 109.)
24 shucked yearling oysters (about 1 pint)
½ cup chopped green onion

Cook pasta al dente, rinse in cold water, drain and reserve. Return a pot of water to the stove, put a colander in it and bring water to a boil.
    Sauté prawns in ½ the butter over medium heat for 2 minutes. Turn prawns, add stock, garlic, cajun spice and oysters. Simmer for 1 minute.
    Meanwhile, put pasta in colander in boiling water for 1 minute. Remove and add pasta to the sauce. Add green onion and remaining butter and toss continually until the butter is melted and everything is well blended.

Approximate preparation time: 15 minutes.

◄ *Fisherman's Fettucini*

Northwest Specialties

The culinary heritage of the Pacific Northwest has never been codified in a list of recipes labeled "Regional Cuisine." Instead, this area's culinary identity has been established by the truly superior array of natural ingredients harvested from its fields and waters.

We are very proud of our roots in the Northwest and have always specialized in dishes that take full advantage of this bounty. When the world's finest salmon, halibut, sturgeon, crab, berries, apples, pears and hazelnuts are found in your own backyard, this is the obvious approach. As professionals, it is an incredible luxury to have immediate access to such wonderful foods.

However, one of our greatest challenges is to present them in ways that highlight, rather than mask, their natural flavors. In most instances, less is more, an attitude wholly compatible with our philosophy of simplicity, clarity and straightforwardness. We think you'll find that this approach works equally well in your kitchen at home.

◀ *Broiled Halibut with Hazelnut-Lemon Butter at the Harborside in Portland. Recipe on page 62.*

CRAB LEG SAUTÉ IN CRANBERRY ORANGE BEURRE BLANC

This is one of the recipes that earned Senior Chef Bill King the title of Oregon Seafood Chef of the Year in 1988. The use of the spaghetti squash as an accompaniment makes an easy yet striking presentation.

Serves 2.

½ cup beurre blanc (See recipe, page 106.)
1 orange, juice and segments
2 cups cooked spaghetti squash
Pinch salt
2 tablespoons butter
8 ounces dungeness crab leg meat
12 whole hazelnuts, toasted and peeled
2 tablespoons avocado balls, scooped with a
    melon baller
3 tablespoons whole cranberries cooked in a little
    water until they pop

Preheat oven to 350°.
    Prepare beurre blanc and reserve.
    Using a sharp paring knife, peel the orange making sure to remove all of the white pith. Cut the orange segments from between the membranes and reserve. Then squeeze what is left of the orange and its membranes to extract the juice. Reserve the juice and segments.
    To cook spaghetti squash: split 1 squash lengthwise and scrape out the seeds. Place it in a baking dish, cut-side down, add 1 cup water and bake for 1 hour or until soft. Remove and run slow running cold water over the cooked squash to cool. Drain, cut-side down on a towel.
    When the squash has cooled and drained, use a dinner fork to scrape the pulp out. It will string and look like golden strands of thin spaghetti.
    Place 2 cups of the cooked squash in a baking dish, sprinkle with salt and dot with 1 tablespoon butter. Put in oven to heat while you prepare the crab.
    Melt 1 tablespoon of butter in a sauté pan over medium heat. Add crab legs and hazelnuts. Heat for 1 minute. Add avocado, orange segments, orange juice and cranberries. Cook for 30 seconds and remove from heat.
    Add beurre blanc and swirl to blend. Do not reheat.
    Remove squash and create nests on two dinner plates. Spoon crab into the center of each nest and arrange some of the cranberries and hazelnuts on the squash as a garnish. Pour the sauce over all.

Approximate preparation time: 1½ hours to cook and cool the squash; 20 minutes for the remainder of the preparation.

BROILED HALIBUT WITH HAZELNUT-LEMON BUTTER

The first halibut of the season is always a treat. Fresh halibut is best served simply so its flavor is showcased. This compound butter from Chef Billy Hahn does just that, while adding a little extra Northwest flavor.

Serves 4.

¼ pound butter, softened
1 teaspoon minced shallots
¼ cup hazelnuts, toasted, peeled and finely chopped
2 tablespoons lemon juice
4 halibut filets or steaks, 6 to 8 ounces each

Combine the butter, shallots, hazelnuts and lemon juice for a compound butter. (See technique described in recipe, page 107.)
    Grill, broil or bake the halibut for 6 to 8 minutes, until opaque and just cooked through. Set on dinner plates and top with the butter.

Approximate preparation time: 2 hours to freeze the butter; 20 minutes to prepare the dish.

Crab Leg Sauté in Cranberry Orange Beurre Blanc ▶

BAKED OYSTERS MELANIE

Senior Chef Marcel Lahsene of Jake's Famous Crawfish Restaurant in Portland created this wonderful oyster dish in honor of Melanie Schmick, wife of co-owner Doug Schmick. The champagne, brie and dill are an inspired combination for a lovely lady. If oyster shucking isn't your thing, have your seafood market do it for you, reserving the meat, nectar and bottom shells.

Serves 4.

½ cup champagne
1 cup cream
1 tablespoon flour
2 tablespoons butter, at room temperature but still
    somewhat firm
Lemon and dill sprigs for garnish
Pinch salt
24 shucked oysters with nectar and bottom shells
4 cups rock salt or kosher salt
12 ounces brie, cut into 24 slices, each ⅛" thick and
    big enough to top an oyster
2 teaspoons fresh chopped dill

Preheat oven to 400°.
    Combine champagne and cream in a saucepan. Reduce over medium heat to about 1 cup. Blend the flour into the butter and add mixture a little at a time to the champagne cream, stirring constantly until the mixture thickens. Season with a pinch of salt and the chopped dill.
    Remove the sauce from the heat and reserve.
    Heat oysters and their nectar in a sauté pan until the edges begin to curl.
    Spread half the rock salt on a baking sheet and arrange the oyster shells on the salt. The salt will help distribute the heat and keep the oysters from tipping over.
    Put an oyster in each of the shells, spoon 2 teaspoons of sauce over each and top with a slice of brie.
    Bake oysters for 3 to 5 minutes or until the sauce is bubbly and the cheese is melted and a little browned.
    For a nice presentation, place a folded napkin on each of four dinner plates and spread remaining salt over the napkins.
    Arrange oysters on the serving plates and garnish with lemon and fresh dill sprigs.

Approximate preparation time: 15 minutes to shuck oysters; 10 minutes to prepare and bake the dish.

NOTE: You'll have the better part of a bottle of champagne left over. Drink it with the oysters. They're made for each other.

NORTHWEST SALMON SAUTÉ

The ultimate Northwest recipe? We're not sure there is one, but if ever there was a dish that represented the finest ingredients the region has to offer, this is it. It is the creation of Chef Joe Gonzales at McCormick's Fish House in Seattle. Wild chanterelle mushrooms are becoming more readily available in grocery stores every year.

Serves 2.

1 cup sliced chanterelles
8 ounces chinook salmon, cut into 1" cubes
2 tablespoons butter
1 teaspoon chopped shallots
1½ tablespoons lemon juice
½ cup cream
4 tablespoons pureed fresh or frozen marionberries or
    other blackberries
2 tablespoons chopped, toasted and peeled hazelnuts

Melt butter over high heat and sauté chanterelles for 1 minute. Add salmon chunks and sauté 1 minute.
    Add all remaining ingredients except the hazelnuts and simmer for 2 minutes, or until sauté has thickened slightly.
    Serve sprinkled with chopped hazelnuts.

Approximate preparation time: 15 minutes.

Baked Oysters Melanie ▶

DUNGENESS CRAB CAKES

There are as many recipes for crab cakes as there are chefs. This one takes the straightforward approach, which we think is best. Try not to break up the crab meat too much while you're mixing. The texture will be better if the crab is chunky.

Makes 8 cakes, 3½" in diameter, or 30 to 40 mini cakes for hors d'oeuvres.

1½ pounds crab meat, picked over for shell
1 cup plain bread crumbs
2 celery stalks, finely minced
1 small onion, finely minced
1 small green pepper, finely minced
1 teaspoon dry mustard
½ teaspoon Tabasco
1 large egg
¼ cup mayonnaise
1 tablespoon lemon juice
½ teaspoon Worcestershire sauce
Additional bread crumbs for coating the crab cakes
½ cup oil for frying (or more)
1 cup tartar sauce or jalapeño hollandaise
    (See recipe, page 107 and 108.)

Preheat oven to 200°.
    Combine all the ingredients except the bread crumbs for coating, the oil and the tartar sauce.
    Form the mixture into 8, 3" to 3½" by 1" thick crab cakes or 30 to 40 hors d'oeuvres.
    Coat cakes on both sides with the additional bread crumbs, patting the crumbs lightly into cakes.
    If you are making large cakes, put about ¼ cup oil into a 10" to 12" sauté pan and cook over medium heat. Cook 4 cakes at a time, 4 minutes per side. They should be nicely browned on both sides and heated through.
    Keep the 4 cooked cakes warm in the oven while you prepare the remaining 4. Use fresh oil for the second batch.

If you're making mini cakes, put the entire ½ cup oil in the sauté pan and fry 10 to 15 at a time, turning once until dark brown. You may need to replace the oil once between batches. Keep cooked mini cakes warm in oven while you cook the rest.

Approximate preparation time: 45 minutes.

RAINBOW TROUT STUFFED WITH BRIE AND APPLES

Chef Steve Vice of Jake's Famous Crawfish Restaurant in Portland cautions that the breading process in this recipe is a little bit tricky. Care must be taken to keep the stuffing inside the fish. Actually, you can simply stuff the trout and bake it, but the crunchy coating adds a lot to the appearance and texture. Make sure to have your fish butcher remove all bones from the trout, and then check that he has.

Serves 2.

2 boneless trout, 8 to 10 ounces each
½ tart green apple, peeled and diced
1 teaspoon butter
1 tablespoon brandy
3 ounces brie, diced small
1 cup flour
1 egg beaten with 1 tablespoon milk
2 cups bread crumbs
¼ cup sour cream
1 tablespoon prepared horseradish
2 tablespoons peeled and finely diced apple
1 tablespoon cream or milk
¼ cup oil for frying

Rinse trout under cold running water and scrape off any remaining scales. Remove heads if you prefer.
    Sauté the apple in the butter and brandy, until the brandy evaporates and the apples soften a bit. Allow apples to cool for a few minutes.

Combine apples and brie and fill cavities of fish.

Set up 3 baking dishes on your counter. Place flour in the first, the egg beaten with milk in the second and the bread crumbs in the third pan.

Hold the fish so the stuffing doesn't fall out, coat the fish one at a time lightly in the flour, shaking off any excess. Dip the fish in the egg, coating it completely. Roll fish in the bread crumbs, pressing them into both sides of the trout. At this point, refrigerate fish for an hour. It helps the breading adhere to the fish.

Preheat oven to 350°.

Meanwhile, combine sour cream, horseradish, apple and cream in a blender and puree until smooth. Reserve.

Heat frying oil in a sauté pan big enough to hold both fish over medium high heat. Add fish and cook for 3 minutes, or until each side is brown.

Remove to a baking dish and bake for 5 minutes. Serve with sauce on the side.

Approximate preparation time: 1½ hours.

LING COD WITH LEMON, CAPERS AND DEMI-BUTTER SAUCE

At McCormick & Schmick's in Seattle, Chef Chris Keff prepares this dish using halibut cheeks. These are extremely sweet and provide counterpoint to the tartness of the sauce. Halibut cheeks are not readily available in retail markets, but the sweet meat of good quality ling cod makes an admirable substitute.

Serves 2.

SAUCE
2 tablespoons lemon juice
2 tablespoons dry white wine
1 tablespoon chopped shallots
2 tablespoons demi-glaze or brown sauce, homemade or commercially prepared (See NOTE.)
¼ pound butter, cold, cut into small cubes

GARNISH
2 tablespoons chopped lemon segments, peeled, seeded, pith removed
2 tablespoons capers
1 piece carrot, 2" long, peeled and cut julienne
2 green onions, white portion cut into 2" julienne, green portion finely chopped
2 ling cod filets, each 6 ounces, each cut into 5 "fingers"
Flour for dusting
Butter or margarine for frying

Combine the lemon juice, white wine and shallots for the sauce and reduce over medium heat until only 2 teaspoons remain. Add the demi-glaze and heat for 2 minutes.

Remove from heat and add the butter, a little at a time, stirring to melt and incorporate.

Assemble all the remaining items.

Dust the fish pieces with flour and sauté in a little butter or margarine for 3 to 4 minutes, until browned and cooked through.

Arrange the fish on dinner plates, spoon the sauce over the fish or on the plate alongside it and sprinkle all the garnish items over the top of the fish and the sauce.

Approximate preparation time: 20 minutes.

NOTE: Demi-glaze is a refinement on the traditional brown sauce used by many professional chefs. It is available in the gourmet section of some supermarkets. A good quality brown or espagnole sauce, either homemade or commercial, makes an adequate substitute.

GRILLED HALIBUT WITH ZINFANDEL SAUCE

This unusual sauce evokes the mulled wine served over the winter holidays. Made by Chef Chris Keff at McCormick & Schmick's in Seattle, it is rich and full of interesting flavors and has no fat. Our restaurants generally cut halibut into filets, but most of the halibut sold in retail outlets is cut into 1" steaks. Either way, the fish is simply grilled or barbecued during the summer season when it is fresh.

Serves 2.

1 bottle Zinfandel wine
1 cup chopped onion
1 bay leaf
4 black peppercorns
1 cinnamon stick
2 cloves
3 garlic cloves
2 halibut filets or steaks, 6 to 8 ounces each

Preheat the grill or barbecue.
    Combine all ingredients, except halibut, in a saucepan and reduce over high heat by half.
    Remove the bay leaf and cinnamon stick and pour the sauce into the bowl of a blender or food processor. Puree for several minutes. The solids should be very well pureed and blended in the sauce.
    Return the sauce to medium heat and reduce for another 5 minutes.
    Meanwhile, cook halibut for 4 minutes per side, or until halibut is just cooked through.
    Remove to dinner plates and pour the sauce over the fish or pool the sauce and place halibut on top.

Approximate preparation time: 30 minutes.

COD CAKES WITH FRESH APPLESAUCE

Cod cakes are an old standby from the fish houses of New England. From the kitchen of Chef Ken Hayes of McCormick & Schmick's in Portland comes the inspired touch of a warm, chunky applesauce. Cook the cod the night before and this recipe comes together quickly.

Makes 4 cakes, 3½" x 1" each.

1 pound true cod or ling cod, poached and cooled
1 stalk celery, finely diced
½ small onion, finely diced (about ¼ cup)
½ teaspoon thyme
¼ teaspoon minced garlic
Pinch salt
Pinch pepper
1 egg
2 tablespoons mayonnaise
1 cup bread crumbs
2 tablespoons butter
2 tart green apples, peeled and diced (about 3 cups)
1 tablespoon lemon juice
½ cup water
3 tablespoons sugar
½ teaspoon cinnamon
3 tablespoons oil for frying

Flake the cod and combine with the next 8 ingredients. Blend well and shape into 4 cakes, 3½" wide by 1" thick .
    Pat and press bread crumbs into the cakes. While you prepare the applesauce, chill the cakes in the refrigerator.
    Melt butter in a sauté pan and add apples, lemon juice, water, sugar and cinnamon. Cook over high heat until the liquids evaporate and the apples soften. Set aside.
    Heat oil in another sauté pan over medium heat and fry the cod cakes for 4 minutes per side until they are crisp, brown and heated through.
    Serve with the applesauce on the side.

Approximate preparation time: 40 minutes.

◄ *Grilled Halibut with Zinfandel Sauce*

JAKE'S DUNGENESS CRAB LEG SAUTÉ

This is one of the best known and most popular dishes prepared by our restaurants. As the name suggests, it hails from our flagship in Portland. Variations on this dish are prepared in all our restaurants, but this is the original, published here for the first time.

Serves 2.

¼ cup béarnaise sauce (See recipe, page 108.)
3 tablespoons butter
10 to 12 mushrooms, sliced (about 1¼ cups)
2 teaspoons minced garlic
4 artichoke hearts, cut in half
4 green onions, chopped (about 4 tablespoons)
¼ cup sherry
Salt and pepper to taste
8 ounces dungeness crab leg meat

Prepare béarnaise sauce and reserve.
    Melt 2 tablespoons of the butter in a sauté pan over medium to high heat and sauté mushrooms for 1 minute. Add garlic, artichoke hearts and green onions. Continue sautéing for another minute. Add sherry, salt and pepper and simmer another 3 minutes.
    Divide the mixture into 2 serving casseroles or boats.
    Return the sauté pan to the heat and add remaining butter and the crab legs. Heat for 2 minutes. Spoon the crab legs over the vegetables and top each boat with 1 to 2 tablespoons of béarnaise.

Approximate preparation time: 10 minutes for the béarnaise sauce; 15 minutes for the sauté.

BRAISED STURGEON WITH DIJON, BASIL AND BALSAMIC VINEGAR

Columbia River sturgeon is one of the most prized of all Northwest seafood. The history and lore of these prehistoric giants would fill pages. Supply has dwindled in recent years, so when you have the opportunity to prepare sturgeon, you want to give it special attention. This recipe from Chef Ken Hayes at McCormick & Schmick's in Portland falls comfortably into that category: truly something special.

Serves 2.

2 sturgeon filets, 6 to 8 ounces each
Flour to dust
2 tablespoons oil for frying
2 tablespoons each, minced carrot, onion, celery and
    red pepper
¼ cup sherry
¼ cup balsamic vinegar
1 teaspoon minced shallots
2 tablespoons dijon mustard
2 tablespoons shredded fresh basil
Pinch salt and pepper
1 tablespoon butter

Lightly flour the sturgeon and brown in the oil over medium-high heat for 2 minutes per side.
    Add the minced vegetables, sherry and vinegar to the pan. Reduce the heat to low, cover the pan and continue cooking for another 3 to 4 minutes, until the vegetables soften and the liquid is reduced by half.
    Add the shallots, mustard, basil, salt and pepper.
    Remove the filets to dinner plates. With the sauté pan off the heat, swirl the butter into the sauce. Then pour the sauce over the fish.

Approximate preparation time: 15 minutes.

BAKED HALIBUT WITH CRAB AND BRIE

Here's the recipe for a dish Bill McCormick once called "one of the most perfect meals I've ever had." He enjoyed it at McCormick & Schmick's in Portland. For all its glory, it's really very easy to prepare. Just a few ingredients blend together perfectly.

Serves 4.

1 cup beurre blanc sauce (See recipe, page 106.)
4 halibut filets (not steaks), 5 ounces each
6 ounces dungeness crab meat
6 ounces bay shrimp
6 ounces brie, cut into ½" cubes
3 tablespoons mayonnaise
1 tablespoon fresh dill, chopped
Pinch salt and pepper

Preheat the oven to 400°.
    Prepare the beurre blanc sauce and reserve.
    Split the halibut filets lengthwise to form a pocket for the stuffing.
    Combine the crab, shrimp, brie, dill, salt and pepper. Gently blend in the mayonnaise to bind the mixture.
    Divide the stuffing mixture between the four pocketed filets. When full, let the flaps cover the stuffing so that only a small amount is exposed.
    Bake in a lightly buttered baking dish for 10 to 12 minutes. Remove to dinner plates and spoon the beurre blanc over the fish.

Approximate preparation time: 30 minutes.

STARK STREET STURGEON

Jake's Famous Crawfish Restaurant in Portland has stood at the corner of 12th and Stark streets for most of its one hundred years. We're not sure whether the location has ever been honored with a dish in its name, but if Stark Street were never famous for anything else, Senior Chef Marcel Lahsene's sturgeon would secure its place in the culinary history of Portland.

Serves 2.

½ cup beurre blanc sauce (See recipe, page 106.)
6 medallions of sturgeon, 2 to 3 ounces each
Flour to dust
Oil for frying
2 tablespoons chopped fresh basil
1 tablespoon dijon mustard
1 teaspoon cracked black peppercorns

Prepare the beurre blanc and reserve.
    Dust sturgeon medallions with flour.
    Cook the sturgeon in a small amount of oil over high heat to sear and brown. This should require no more than 1 to 2 minutes per side. Reduce heat to low, pour off the excess oil and add the beurre blanc, basil, mustard and pepper.
    Swirl to blend the sauce and coat the medallions.

Approximate preparation time: 20 minutes.

GRILLED FILET OF KING SALMON

Simplicity can be a very complex concept to address. Take, for example, the filet of salmon, pictured on page 72. It appears to be a very simple, straightforward piece of grilled fish. In fact, the final preparation is the result of many decisions. First, what kind of salmon is it? Where, when, how, and by whom was it caught? Second, how was it handled by its distributors? Third, what is the best way to showcase its flavor, what sauce or vegetable will accompany it best? All this has to be decided before your fish even touches a hot grill.

For tips to help make the right selections at the seafood counter, turn to page 106. For proper cooking techniques, read on. But remember, there is nothing simple about it!

Serves 4.

4 filets of fresh king or chinook salmon, 6 to 8 ounces
    each, approximately 1" thick
Oil to coat fish

Make sure that your filets are free from all bones and that the flesh is firm and intact.

Prepare the barbecue or preheat the rangetop grill to medium high heat. Make sure that the grill grates, not just the fire itself, are hot.

Brush the grates with a little vegetable oil. The oil, along with the hot temperature of the grates, will prevent the fish from sticking and assure proper grill markings on the salmon.

Coat the salmon lightly with vegetable oil and place on the grill so that the longest dimension of the filet is at a 45 degree angle to the grill pattern.

If you like your salmon as we do, cooked medium to medium rare with a pink center, "mark" the fish by rotating it another 45 degrees after approximately 2 minutes. After 2 more minutes, flip the filet over and grill on the other side for an additional 4 minutes. The salmon should be just barely cooked through with a medium pink center and lightly charred with grill marks.

Prepared in this fashion, the salmon's naturally rich and distinctive flavor will be highlighted. However, there are a few acceptable variations:

▶ Serve accompanied by a beurre blanc sauce infused with the flavors of blackberry or orange. (See recipe, page 106.)

▶ Rub the filet with lemon juice and chopped fresh dill prior to grilling.

▶ For a distinctively Northwest flavor, slow the fire down to medium high and sprinkle dampened alderwood chips on your barbecue coals. Prepared in this manner, the salmon will take on a faintly smoky flavor reminiscent of the alder-smoked salmon prepared for centuries by Northwest Indians.

NOTE: Chinook is the traditional Indian name for the Pacific king salmon. Although red king salmon is by far the most prominent, white kings, usually from Alaska, are also available from time to time. Their ivory flesh and rich flavor make them highly sought after by knowledgeable Northwest diners.

◀ *Grilled Filet of King Salmon*

Shellfish

There are two basic species of shellfish: mollusks, represented by oysters, clams, mussels and the like; and crustaceans, long regarded as the royal family of seafood. Lobster, crab, jumbo shrimp and prawns all conjure images of elegant dinners and special occasions where caution (and your checkbook) are thrown to the wind.

Although there is an element of truth to this attitude, it's no reason to deprive yourself of the luscious, sweet flavors that these creatures possess. In our restaurants, we generally take two different approaches. When our intent is to provide a simple, straightforward preparation, steaming is the method most frequently employed. Whether it is a large dungeness crab, a whole Maine lobster or a heaping bowl of Manila clams, mussels or pink "singing" scallops, they arrive at the table preceded by the sweet, steaming aroma of their nectar, and accompanied by nothing more than the broth itself and a little drawn butter for dipping.

The other style of preparation that lends itself well to shellfish cookery is sautéing. The key to success here is to have all ingredients ready at the stove—what the French call *mis en place*. Organized in this fashion, glorious shellfish preparations are just moments away, as you will find when you try our recipes.

◄ *Sea Scallops with Roasted Garlic Sauce at McCormick & Schmick's in Seattle. Recipe on page 81.*

ALMOND PRAWNS WITH PAPAYA BUTTER

This dish is always one of our biggest sellers when it's on the menu at McCormick & Schmick's in Portland. Prepare this dish only when the papaya is very ripe and flavorful.

Serves 4.

24 jumbo prawns, peeled and deveined
¼ cup salad oil
1 cup blanched, sliced or slivered almonds
4 tablespoons butter, softened to room temperature
1 papaya
Pinch salt
1 teaspoon curry powder

Preheat oven to 450°.
    Cut prawns lengthwise from top to tail almost all the way through. This procedure is called butterflying. The prawns should spread flat without separating.
    Coat prawns lightly in about half of oil.
    Chop blanched almonds until they are very fine. If you do this in a blender or food processor, be careful you don't go too far or you'll end up with nut butter. Spread chopped nuts in a large baking dish or on a cookie sheet.
    Coat prawns with the nuts and refrigerate for 5 minutes. Cut the papaya in half and remove the seeds. Scoop out the papaya pulp and puree along with the butter, salt and curry powder until smooth. If the papaya and butter do not blend completely and the mixture appears grainy, place it in a saucepan and stir it constantly over high heat for 15 to 20 seconds. (The blend will come together very quickly. If you heat it too long, the butter will separate.)
    Coat a baking sheet with the remaining oil and preheat it in the oven for 2 to 3 minutes. Remove the pan from the oven and place the prawns on it and return to oven.
    Cook prawns for 5 to 6 minutes, turning once, until they are browned and firm to the touch.
    Place prawns on plates and top with papaya butter.

Approximate preparation time: 30 to 40 minutes.

ROCK SHRIMP, CRAB AND CHANTERELLE SAUTÉ IN PUFF PASTRY

This recipe is representative of the many sauté dishes we serve in our restaurants. A little of this, a little of that, and some great fresh quality seafood finished with beurre blanc. What you end up with is clearly more than the sum of its parts. Chef Whitney Peterson of McCormick's Fish House in Beaverton, Oregon, serves this in a puff pastry shell for a striking presentation.

Serves 2.

2 frozen puff pastry shells or fresh, homemade puff pastry
2 tablespoons butter
1½ cups sliced chanterelles
8 ounces rock shrimp
2 teaspoons chopped shallots
⅔ cup fish bouillon or chicken stock
⅔ cup sherry
¾ cup beurre blanc (See recipe, page 108.)
Salt and pepper to taste
2 tablespoons chopped parsley

Prepare the puff pastry or bake frozen shells according to package instructions.
    Melt butter in a sauté pan over medium high heat and sauté the chanterelles for 1 minute, until they begin to soften. Add rock shrimp and shallots and sauté an additional 2 minutes. Add bouillon and sherry and simmer for another 2 minutes. Season with salt and pepper.
    Remove from heat and swirl in the beurre blanc, then spoon the sauce over the puff pastry and sprinkle with chopped parsley.

Approximate preparation time: 20 minutes.

Almond Prawns with Papaya Butter ▶

CURRIED SCALLOPS

Chef David Holly of McCormick & Schmick's on Pacific Beach in San Diego uses giant sea scallops for this recipe and creates a visually striking meal. Sea scallops are not often available in retail markets. If you find some, this is a great recipe to try. As an option, we offer the recipe using bay scallops as well. If you like curry, you'll enjoy this dish.

Serves 2.

1 tablespoon butter
1 tablespoon finely diced onion
1 tablespoon flour
1 teaspoon curry powder
½ cup chicken stock
½ cup cream
1 teaspoon orange zest
Pinch saffron
12 jumbo sea scallops (10 to 20 or 20 to 30 per pound) or
     12 ounces bay scallops
2 tablespoons butter, if you're using sea scallops

Melt butter over medium heat and sauté onions until they soften. Add flour and curry powder to form a roux. Add stock, cream, zest and saffron and simmer until lightly thickened.

    If you're using bay scallops, add them to the sauce at this time and simmer for 2 to 3 minutes to cook. If you're using sea scallops, cook the sauce for an additional 2 to 3 minutes, then reserve, keeping the sauce warm.

    Flour sea scallops lightly. Melt an additional 2 tablespoons butter in another sauté pan over medium-high heat and sauté sea scallops for 3 to 4 minutes, turning once, until golden brown.

    Arrange sea scallops on plate and pour the curry sauce over them.

Approximate preparation time: 15 minutes.

PRAWNS WITH ROSEMARY AND CRACKED BLACK PEPPER

This is a relatively new addition to the menu of Jake's Famous Crawfish Restaurant from Chef Steve Vice. Full of assertive flavors, it has become a customer favorite. Use fresh rosemary if you can. If not, let the dried rosemary soak in the beer for several minutes before preparing the dish.

Serves 2.

12 jumbo prawns, peeled and deveined
2 tablespoons cracked black pepper, freshly ground
2 teaspoons rosemary
2 teaspoons Worcestershire sauce
1 cup beer
2 teaspoons cajun magic or homemade cajun spice
     (See recipe, page 109.)
5 tablespoons butter
2 teaspoons minced garlic
1 tablespoon chopped parsley

Lay the peeled prawns on a plate and generously grind pepper over both sides.

    Combine rosemary, Worcestershire, beer and cajun spice and reserve.

    Melt half the butter in a large sauté pan over medium heat and add prawns. Cook 2 minutes. The prawns will curl and begin to turn opaque.

    Flip the prawns and add the beer mixture and garlic. Continue cooking for another 2 minutes.

    Remove prawns to dinner plates and return the sauce to heat to reduce for 3 to 4 minutes. Remove from heat, swirl in the remaining butter and pour over prawns.

Approximate preparation time: 20 minutes.

Curried Scallops ▶

SEA SCALLOPS with ROASTED GARLIC SAUCE

When all our chefs get together two or three times a year, one of the dishes we most enjoy is the creation of Chef Chris Keff of McCormick & Schmick's in Seattle. Use sea scallops, sized 10 to 20 per pound, not the smaller bay scallops.

Serves 4.

4 heads garlic
2 tablespoons chopped shallots
¾ cup dry white wine
2 tablespoons white wine vinegar
¼ cup cream
½ pound butter, cut into small cubes, kept cold
2 tablespoons butter for frying
24 jumbo sea scallops
½ cup flour to dust scallops
2 tablespoons chopped chives

Preheat oven to 350°.
    Keep heads of garlic whole, but peel off the loose outside skins. Coat with a drizzle of oil. Bake garlic for 1 hour, or until the cloves feel soft. Allow garlic to cool.
    Separate cloves and squeeze out the softened garlic pulp. Combine with shallots, wine and vinegar and simmer over medium heat for 15 minutes, or until the liquid has just about disappeared. Add cream and continue to reduce for another 3 to 5 minutes.
    Remove the sauce from heat and add butter a little at a time, stirring constantly, waiting between additions for the butter to melt into the sauce. If you find butter failing to melt, return the sauce to very low heat just until melting begins again. Once all the butter is melted and blended, remove sauce to the side of the stove and keep warm.
    Dust the scallops in flour and shake off any excess. Heat butter in a sauté pan over medium heat. Add scallops and brown them for 2 to 3 minutes on each side.
    Pour some of the sauce on each of four dinner plates and arrange 6 scallops in each pool of sauce.

Sprinkle with chopped chives to garnish.

Approximate preparation time: 1 hour to bake garlic; 30 minutes to prepare.

PRAWN and SEA SCALLOP BROCHETTE

Brochettes are a popular way to present foods, and they make grilled or broiled shellfish easy to handle. Baste with this barbecue sauce from Chef Joe Gonzales for great summer entertaining.

Makes 2 large brochettes.

½ cup mango chutney (Major Grey's brand)
½ cup orange juice
¼ cup barbecue sauce, homemade or commercial
6 large prawns, peeled and deveined
6 large sea scallops
4 pineapple chunks
4 tomato chunks
4 onion chunks
Bamboo or metal skewers

Prepare the barbecue glaze by combining the chutney, orange juice and barbecue sauce and blending thoroughly.
    Preheat the grill.
    Start each brochette with a pineapple chunk.
    Place a sea scallop inside the curve of a prawn and pierce with a skewer so the prawn wraps around the scallop.
    Complete the first series with a chunk of tomato and a chunk of onion. Repeat the process with another shrimp, scallop, tomato and onion and finish the skewer with a third shrimp and scallop and a second pineapple chunk.
    Repeat the process with the second skewer.
    Brush the brochettes with ½ the barbecue sauce and broil or grill for 5 to 6 minutes, basting with additional sauce and turning as needed, until the shrimp and scallops are opaque and firm to the touch.

Approximate preparation time: 20 minutes.

◀ *Prawn and Sea Scallop Brochette*

Seafood

It wasn't long ago that the number of fresh seafood species available at retail markets could be counted on one hand. There was always some kind of sole, a rockfish incorrectly promoted as "snapper" and salmon or halibut, depending on the season. Even at the restaurant level, the selection was extremely limited.

So we started our own distribution company and found access to fine fish from around the world: fresh yellowfin tuna known as ahi, swordfish, several varieties of marlin, mahi mahi and true Pacific snappers with exotic names like uku, lehi and ulua from Hawaii. King mackerel, called ono, opah and a wide assortment of New Zealand species all found their way to our docks and ultimately to our diners.

Over the past few years, the rest of the industry has caught up, and retail fish counters are stocked with an exciting array of fresh seafood year-round. Here are our favorite ways to take advantage of these opportunities.

◀ *Sole Parmesan at McCormick's Fish House in Beaverton. Recipe on page 86.*

SEAFOOD STIR-FRY

It doesn't take a wok to produce a good stir-fry. The key is brief cooking times and constant motion. This stir-fry can use any combination of ingredients that suit your taste and the contents of your refrigerator. This dish is very popular with our lunch customers whenever it is offered.

Serves 4.

3 tablespoons oil
¾ pound seafood: rock shrimp, bay scallops, bay shrimp, 2" chunks of salmon, rockfish, bass, cod (Select at least 2 or 3 items.)
1½ cups julienne carrot (about 2 carrots)
1½ cups julienne red and/or green pepper (about 1 pepper)
1½ cups julienne green onion (about 1 bunch)
1 cup snowpeas, ends trimmed
½ cup sliced water chestnuts
1 tablespoon minced garlic
1 tablespoon minced fresh ginger or 1 teaspoon powdered ginger
½ cup sherry
¼ cup hoisin sauce
1 cup teriyaki sauce
4 cups mung bean sprouts

Trim and cut the seafood and vegetables (except bean sprouts) and assemble by the stovetop.
    Heat oil over high heat in a large sauté pan or wok. Add vegetables and cook for 1 minute. Add seafood, garlic and ginger and cook 1 more minute. Add sherry, hoisin and teriyaki. Stir-fry 1 more minute. When completed, your vegetables should be crisp-tender and the seafood just cooked through. Arrange bean sprouts in a nest on four serving plates and divide the stir-fry among the plates.

Approximate preparation time: 20 minutes.

NOTE: If you like your Chinese food spicy, add 2 tablespoons of Szechuan chili paste to this recipe.

◀ *Seafood Stir-fry*

SWORDFISH PEPPERSTEAK

This recipe from chef David Holly of McCormick and Schmick's in San Diego is inspired by the classic steak *au poivre*. It's a great example of the way in which one recipe gives birth to another in the mind of a creative chef. It's also an example of one of the best swordfish preparations we have ever tasted.

Serves 2.

2 swordfish steaks, 6 to 8 ounces each
2 to 3 tablespoons green peppercorns, drained
3 tablespoons butter
½ cup sliced mushrooms
½ cup tomato, peeled, seeded and diced
3 tablespoons brandy
4 tablespoons cream
Pinch fresh rosemary

Preheat oven to 400°.
    Press the peppercorns into only 1 side of each swordfish steak.
    Melt 2 tablespoons butter in a sauté pan over medium-high heat.
    Place swordfish, pepper-side down, in the pan for 2 minutes to sear. (This will also adhere the peppercorns to the fish.) If a few peppercorns fall off, that's okay. Leave them in the pan for the sauce.
    Remove the swordfish to a baking dish, pepper-side up, and finish in the oven for 5 to 6 minutes.
    Meanwhile, add 1 tablespoon butter to the sauté pan and sauté mushrooms for 1 minute. Add diced tomato and cook for 30 seconds on medium heat. Add brandy and cook for another 30 seconds. Then add cream and rosemary and simmer for 2 to 3 minutes.
    Remove swordfish to dinner plates, pour the sauce over them and serve.

Approximate preparation time: 15 minutes.

SOLE PARMESAN

This dish is a little tricky and may take some practice, but the results are well worth the effort. If you have a range-top system such as a Jenn-Air, the griddle attachment makes things quite a bit easier. The key is getting the Parmesan coating crisp and brown without having it stick to the pan. High heat and a non-stick surface are necessary.

Serves 2.

½ cup flour
1 egg, beaten with 1 tablespoon milk
6 to 8 ounces fresh shredded Parmesan (canned, grated cheese will *not* work)
1 cup flaked, dried bread crumbs
12 to 16 ounces boneless filet of sole (preferably petrale)
3 tablespoons oil for frying
2 tablespoons butter
2 tablespoons lemon juice
6 lemon segments, chopped
2 teaspoons capers
1 teaspoon chopped shallots
1 tablespoon chopped parsley

Place the flour, egg and shredded Parmesan mixed with the bread crumbs in 3 separate baking dishes. (As noted, the Parmesan must be freshly shredded, into thin pieces similar to ½" long toothpicks, *not* grated into granules or a powder.)
    Dip the filets in flour first, shaking off excess, then into egg and finally in the cheese, taking great care to coat the fish evenly and completely.
    Heat the oil in a large non-stick sauté pan or on a range-top griddle over high heat. Place fish in pan and allow to brown, about 1 minute. Turn fish, taking care not to disturb the crisply browned cheese. (If the coating flakes off the fish in spots, retrieve the specks of cheese and scatter them back on top of the fish.) After turning, the fish will take only 1 more minute. Remove to dinner plates.
    Wipe oil from pan and return it to the stove or, if using the griddle, heat a sauté pan. Add remaining ingredients and cook over medium heat until the butter is slightly browned. Pour over fish.

Approximate preparation time: 20 minutes.

NOTE: If the pan is not hot enough or the wrong cheese is used, the coating will gum up and ruin the fish.

ORANGE ROUGHY WITH CANDIED GINGER-KIWI SAUCE

This is a terrific sauce for almost any fish. It's light, fresh, tart, sweet and a little spicy. It's also very easy to prepare and looks wonderful. What more could you ask? We offer it as a topping for orange roughy, an overachiever of a fish whose popularity is a Madison Avenue success story.

Serves 2.

1 kiwi, peeled and diced
1 tablespoon rice wine vinegar
2 tablespoons lime juice
2 teaspoons brown sugar
1½ tablespoons peeled ginger, sliced in 2" julienne strips
½ cup orange juice
2 teaspoons sugar
2 orange roughy filets, 6 to 8 ounces each

Combine the first four ingredients and reserve.
    Combine the next three ingredients in a saucepan and simmer for 10 minutes, or until the mixture is reduced to approximately 3 tablespoons of thickened syrup.
    Combine the kiwi-brown sugar mixture with the ginger-sugar mixture. Grill the fish for 3 to 4 minutes per side and remove to dinner plates. Spoon the sauce over the fish and serve.

Approximate preparation time: 15 minutes.

TUNA with MADEIRA, ORANGE and SOY

This unusual combination of ingredients makes for a surprising and delicious sauce that suits fresh tuna. Madeira is a fortified wine similar to sherry, which can be used as a substitute although it is not quite as full flavored.

Serves 2.

4 medallions of yellowfin tuna, 3 to 4 ounces each
½ cup flour
2 tablespoons salad oil
1 tablespoon soy sauce
¼ cup madeira
¼ cup orange juice
¼ cup cream
2 tablespoons butter

Preheat oven to 200°.
    Dust tuna medallions with flour and shake off excess. Heat oil over medium flame in a sauté pan large enough to hold the medallions. Fry for 2 minutes on each side, until browned. Remove to a holding pan and keep warm in the oven.
    Pour off and wipe out any excess oil from the pan and return to the heat. Combine all remaining ingredients except the butter and boil to reduce by half.
    Remove sauce from heat and swirl in the butter until just melted and blended in the sauce.
    Place tuna medallions on dinner plates and pour sauce over them.

Approximate preparation time: 15 minutes.

SWORDFISH CASINO

Swordfish has become a luxury these days as the price moves out of sight. When you add crab meat, you're likely to break the bank. But if you've got someone you really want to impress, and money's no object, here's a classy recipe from Chef Whitney Petersen at McCormick's Fish House in Beaverton for a very special dinner party.

Serves 2.

¼ cup beurre blanc sauce (See recipe, page 108.)
2 swordfish steaks, 1" thick, 5 to 6 ounces each
3 ounces dungeness crab meat
2 tablespoons roasted red peppers, julienne cut
    (See NOTE.)
1 teaspoon lemon juice
2 tablespoons fresh basil leaves, finely shredded
Pinch salt
Pinch pepper

Preheat oven to 400°
    Prepare the beurre blanc.
    Cut a slit in the swordfish steaks to form a pocket, as you might for stuffed pork chops.
    Combine crab, roasted peppers, lemon, basil and salt and pepper to make the stuffing. Divide between the pockets of the 2 steaks.
    If you have a range-top system like a Jenn-Air, you can "mark" the swordfish with the grill's crosshatching. Marked or not, bake in the oven for 10 minutes.
    Remove to dinner plates and coat each steak with 2 tablespoons beurre blanc.

Approximate preparation time: 20 minutes.

NOTE: Roasted red peppers are readily available in supermarkets.

SEAFOOD CHILI

At first you might be somewhat skeptical about the wisdom of serving chili made with seafood, but don't knock it until you've tried it. This chili from Chef Rene VanBroekhuizen, is great! The flavors blend nicely and it doesn't overpower the fish. Most shellfish and fish work in this recipe, which is great for lunch, dinner or reheated leftovers.

Serves 4 to 6.

1 cup dry black beans
3 tablespoons olive oil
1 cup diced onion
1 cup diced red and/or green pepper
1 small jalapeño, minced
2 teaspoons chipotle pepper puree (See NOTE.)
1 teaspoon cumin
1 teaspoon chili powder
1 teaspoon onion powder
½ teaspoon oregano
½ teaspoon salt
1 teaspoon black pepper
1 cup chicken stock, commercial or homemade
1 28-ounce can diced tomato
1 pound bay shrimp
1½ pounds fish filet (cod, sea bass, rockfish, etc.), diced
8 ounces cheddar or jack cheese, shredded
1 bunch cilantro, chopped or sprigs
Assorted hot or mild peppers, for garnish
1 cup fresh tomato, papaya or avocado salsa
      (See recipe, page 108 & 109.)
6 large flour tortillas, rolled and halved for garnish

Soak the black beans overnight. Drain. Cook the beans in fresh water until tender. Drain and reserve.

Heat 1 tablespoon of the oil. Add the next 10 ingredients and cook over medium heat for 4 to 5 minutes. Add the chicken stock and tomatoes, reduce the heat to low and simmer 20 minutes.

Heat the remaining olive oil in another saucepan and sauté the seafood for 2 to 3 minutes.

Add the chili sauce and black beans to the seafood and cook an additional 1 to 2 minutes.

Spoon the chili into bowls and top with the cheese. Garnish with the cilantro, peppers, salsa and flour tortillas.

Approximately preparation time: Soak beans overnight; 1 hour preparation time.

NOTE: Canned chipotle peppers are available in specialty and Mexican groceries. Oriental hot chili paste also works.

GRILLED MAHI MAHI WITH MANGO-ORANGE BARBECUE GLAZE

From the repertoire of Chef Joe Gonzales, this terrific barbecue baste can be used on several types of seafood. (See Prawn and Sea Scallop Brochette in Shellfish section.) If you have a favorite recipe for homemade barbecue sauce, use it or pick your favorite commercial brand.

Serves 4.

1 cup mango chutney (Major Grey's brand)
1 cup orange juice
½ cup barbecue sauce, homemade or commercial
4 mahi mahi filets, 4 to 6 ounces each
Oil to coat fish

Combine chutney, orange juice and barbecue sauce in a blender and puree until the solids in the chutney are smooth.

Barbecue the mahi mahi over a medium high fire, 3 to 4 minutes per side, basting frequently with sauce, until the filets are just cooked through. Glaze the top of the filets with extra sauce as they come off the fire.

Approximate preparation time: 15 minutes.

◀ *Seafood Chili*

TUNA BRAISED WITH CRANBERRIES, PORT AND CREAM

Created at Jake's Famous Crawfish Restaurant, this dish features a full-flavored sauce that stands up to the rich meaty flavor of fresh tuna. When buying fresh tuna, look for dark purple color and a bright, glossy finish. The best yellowfin tuna, called ahi, comes from Hawaii.

Serves 2.

2 tuna steaks, 6 to 8 ounces each, 1" thick
Flour to dust the tuna
3 tablespoons butter
½ cup port
2 tablespoons finely minced shallots
¼ cup whole cranberry sauce
2 tablespoons demi-glaze or brown sauce (See NOTE.)
Zest from ½ orange, finely julienne
¼ cup cream

Dust tuna steaks lightly with flour.
　　Melt ½ the butter over medium-high heat.
　　Pan-fry the tuna for 1 minute on each side or until brown. Remove the fish and increase the heat to high.
　　Deglaze the pan by pouring in the port. Add the shallots, cranberry sauce, demiglaze and orange zest and bring to a boil. Reduce the heat to simmer and add cream.
　　Return the tuna steaks to braise for 4 minutes.
　　Remove tuna to dinner plates and continue to reduce the sauce for an additional 2 to 3 minutes. Swirl in the remaining butter and pour the sauce over the tuna.

Approximate preparation time: 20 minutes.

NOTE: Demi-glaze is a refinement on the brown sauce used by professional chefs. It is available in the gourmet section of some supermarkets. A quality brown or espagnol sauce, homemade or commercial, may be substituted.

PECAN CATFISH WITH HONEY LEMON CHILI BUTTER

Using chopped nuts to coat fish before cooking is a great way to add flavor and texture to your meal. When pan-frying a nut-coated fish, you must take care to keep the heat moderate so you don't burn it. Chef Whitney Peterson of McCormick's Fish House in Beaverton, Oregon, finishes this fish with a trio of sweet, tart and spicy flavors.

Serves 2.

2 catfish filets, 6 to 8 ounces each
1 cup pecans
1 cup flour
1 egg beaten with 1 tablespoon milk
3 tablespoons oil for frying
4 tablespoons chicken stock
1 tablespoon honey
1 tablespoon lemon juice
¼ teaspoon crushed red chili pepper flakes
1 tablespoon melted butter
1 teaspoon chopped parsley

Trim any loose pieces from the catfish filets.
　　Chop the pecans very fine.
　　Set up 3 baking dishes or pie pans on your counter and put flour in the first pan, beaten egg in the second and chopped pecans in the third.
　　Bread the filets by coating lightly in flour, shaking off the excess. Dip them in the egg and finally coat them in the nuts, pressing the pecans into the filets on both sides.
　　Heat 3 tablespoons of oil in a large pan.
　　Combine the remaining ingredients for the sauce.
　　Pan-fry the catfish over medium-high heat, for 3 to 4 minutes per side. If the coating gets too brown too quickly, remove filets to a pie pan and finish them in a 400° oven for 3 to 4 minutes.
　　Place the cooked catfish on dinner plates and pour the sauce over them.

Approximate preparation time: 20 minutes.

LING COD WITH SCALLOPS IN TOMATO-BASIL BEURRE BLANC

This is an example of using a simple piece of fish as the foundation for an elaborate dish. Ling cod is the ideal fish to use in this manner. It's light and sweet on its own and combines well with all sorts of other seafood and seasonings. This meal has been a popular one on the menu at McCormick & Schmick's for many years.

Serves 2.

½ cup beurre blanc (See recipe, page 106.)
2 ling cod filets, 4 ounces each
2 tablespoons butter
6 ounces bay scallops
2 teaspoons minced shallots
¼ cup peeled, seeded and diced tomato
¼ cup shredded fresh basil leaves

Preheat oven to 400°.
    Prepare beurre blanc and reserve.
    Place the cod filets in a baking dish and dot with ½ of the butter. Bake cod for 6 to 8 minutes, depending on its thickness, until it begins to flake.
    Meanwhile, prepare scallops by sautéing them over medium heat in the remaining butter for 30 seconds. Add the shallots, tomato and basil. Cook another 30 seconds.
    Remove the pan from the heat and swirl in the beurre blanc. Remove cod filets from oven and arrange on two dinner plates. Spoon scallops and sauce over the filets.

Approximate preparation time: 30 minutes.

BLACKTIP SHARK WITH SZECHUAN VINAIGRETTE

Shark is one of the most popular exotic fish sold in retail markets. It has a mild and meaty flavor but can sometimes be tough, and there's really no way to tell in advance. This sauce would also be excellent for swordfish or fresh tuna and is a great baste for the barbecue.

Serves 2.

2 teaspoons hot chili paste with garlic (Available in
        Oriental department of grocery stores and in
        Oriental markets. Lon Chi is the brand we use.)
2 teaspoons minced cilantro
½ teaspoon ginger powder
1 tablespoon sesame oil
½ tablespoon soy sauce
2 tablespoons rice wine vinegar
2 tablespoons salad oil
1 teaspoon brown sugar
⅓ cup julienne carrot
⅓ cup julienne celery
⅓ cup julienne green onion
Oil or non-stick spray
2 blacktip shark steaks, 6 to 8 ounces each, 1" thick

Preheat the grill.
    To prepare the vinaigrette, combine and blend first 8 ingredients. Add the julienne vegetables and reserve.
    Lightly coat the shark with oil or non-stick spray. Grill for 4 to 5 minutes per side, basting with the vinaigrette.
    Top with the remaining vinaigrette and serve.

Approximate preparation time: 20 minutes.

TUNA "BLACK AND BLEU"

Here's an unusual preparation that, admittedly, may not be for everyone. But those who have tried it at McCormick & Kuleto's in San Francisco have responded with rave reviews. The tuna is coated in a cajun-style spice mixture and seared briefly in a very hot pan. The result is a black exterior and a bleu (the French term for "cooked very rare") interior.

Serves 2.

2 yellowfin tuna filets, very fresh, 6 to 9 ounces each
¼ cup cajun magic or homemade cajun spice
    (See recipe, page 109.)
4 tablespoons butter
1 tablespoon wasabi powder, available at Oriental
    grocery stores
2 tablespoons soy sauce
Non-stick vegetable oil spray

Preheat a cast-iron skillet or sauté pan on high heat. Make sure you have your exhaust fan on.
    Coat both sides of the tuna filets with the cajun spice, shaking off any excess. Combine the butter and wasabi and heat to blend and melt. Place wasabi butter and soy in separate dishes. They will be used as dipping sauces for the tuna.
    Spray both sides of the spice-coated tuna steaks with the non-stick spray and place them in the pan, which by now should be very hot. Sear the fish for 1 minute on each side and serve along with the dip sauces.
    For a dramatic presentation and ease of eating, you might want to carefully carve the seared tuna into very thin slices before bringing it to your table. We've found that this sort of extra touch makes a strong impression on our guests. It will surely do the same for you and yours.

Approximate preparation time: 15 minutes.

◀ *Tuna "Black and Bleu" from McCormick & Kuleto's in San Francisco.*

SEAFOOD ENCHILADA

Chef Rene VanBroekhuizen has real creative flair with ethnic dishes. His menu at McCormick & Schmick's in Irvine was always full of seafood variations on Oriental and Mexican classics. Now at our restaurant in San Francisco's Ghirardelli Square, Rene has brought his creative cuisine to Bay Area residents with equally spectacular results.

Makes 4 small tortillas.

4 tablespoons finely diced onion
1 tablespoon finely diced jalapeño
4 tablespoons finely diced green pepper
2 tablespoons oil
¼ teaspoon salt
¼ teaspoon pepper
¼ teaspoon cayenne
¼ teaspoon oregano
¼ teaspoon minced garlic
¼ teaspoon cumin
⅔ cup cream
12 ounces cheddar and/or jack cheese, shredded
4 small corn or flour tortillas
8 ounces seafood (crab, bay shrimp, cod, rockfish,
    etc.), poached
¼ cup diced green chilies

Preheat oven to 400°.
    Sauté onions and peppers in oil until slightly softened. Add next 7 ingredients along with ⅓ the cheese and simmer to thicken.
    Combine half the remaining cheese with the seafood and green chiles and roll mixture in each of the tortillas.
    Place enchiladas in a baking dish, coat with sauce and sprinkle with remaining cheese. Bake for 15 minutes or until hot, bubbling and lightly browned.
    Serve enchiladas with fresh salsa and black beans.

Approximate preparation time: 30 minutes.

GRILLED MAHI MAHI WITH SOY-SHIITAKE GLAZE

This sweet-tart sauce goes well with exotic fish like tuna, marlin, sailfish and ono. Mahi mahi, one of the most popular specialty fish served in our restaurants, is particularly well suited to the shiitake mushrooms used in the sauce. Shiitake mushrooms are becoming widely available in supermarkets.

Serves 4.

1½ cups dark brown sugar
½ cup soy sauce
2 cups water
Fresh ginger root, 4" long, peeled and chopped
3 green onions, coarsely chopped
¼ lemon
¼ orange
1 tablespoon chopped garlic
4 mahi mahi filets, 6 to 8 ounces each
1 pound shiitake mushrooms, left whole if small; halved
    or quartered if larger
½ cup sesame oil
½ cup sliced green onions

Combine the first 8 ingredients in a saucepan and cook over medium heat for 2 hours. The mixture should reduce down to a thick, syrupy 1 cup. Strain and reserve.

Grill the mahi filets to desired doneness. For a 1" thick filet this should take 4 minutes per side over high heat. Meanwhile, sauté the shiitakes in the sesame oil 2 to 3 minutes, until they begin to soften. Add green onions and continue cooking for 1 more minute.

Add the soy-sugar mixture. Make sure that the sauce doesn't boil over. It will bubble and expand when combined.

Brush a little of the sauce on the fish for the last minute it is cooking. Use the remaining sauce and mushrooms to spoon over the fish on your dinner plates.

Approximate preparation time: 2 hours for the sauce; 10 minutes to cook the fish and complete the dish.

GRILLED ONO WITH THREE-CITRUS MARINADE

This is a versatile marinade for all kinds of grilled fish. In addition it is light and fresh and has zero fat. Prepare it 1 to 2 hours before use to allow flavors to blend. Ono is a member of the mackerel family, but it doesn't have the strong oily taste associated with mackerel. It is one of the most popular "exotic" fish served in our restaurants.

Serves 4.

1 large grapefruit, segments and juice
1 medium lime, segments and juice
2 medium oranges, segments and juice
½ red onion, julienne cut
½ cup rice wine vinegar
1 tablespoon brown sugar
4 ono filets, 6 to 8 ounces each
Oil to coat filets for grilling

Peel and cut segments from the citrus fruits. Squeeze the remaining portions of the fruit to extract the juice. You should have at least ½ cup combined juices.

Combine all the fruit segments, juices, onion, vinegar and sugar. Allow to rest for 1 to 2 hours.

Coat the filets with oil and grill ono filets over high heat for 3 minutes per side, until they are opaque and just cooked through.

Remove fish to a plate and top with the citrus mixture.

Approximate preparation time: 2 hours for the sauce to rest and marry; 6 minutes to grill the fish.

Grilled Ono with Three-Citrus Marinade ▶

Dessert

We've never been a French pastry kind of company. Long before homestyle and comfort foods became buzzwords for trendy restaurants, our dessert trays proudly displayed the kind of cakes, pies and desserts our grandmothers prepared in their home kitchens. We still feel that there's nothing better than a great piece of deep-dish apple pie or a warm, Oregon berry cobbler topped with a scoop of ice cream.

The Pacific Northwest has accommodated our tastes by producing some of the finest fruits and nuts in the world. They're a natural inspiration for our old-fashioned preparations.

Again, like so many of the other dishes in this book, these recipes are relatively easy to prepare at home and don't require a master pastry chef's diploma to execute them. All you need are impeccable ingredients and your grandma's spirit watching over.

◀ *Traditional American Desserts from our Dessert Tray.*

THREE-BERRY COBBLER

This is one of our most popular desserts, an old-fashioned favorite that will please the most jaded of palates. Naturally, it's best when berries are fresh, but we serve it year-round using frozen berries from the summer harvest. Try topping this with vanilla ice cream for the best treat this side of heaven.

Makes 4 custard dishes, each ⅔ cup.

CRUST
1¼ cups flour
1½ teaspoons baking powder
1 tablespoon sugar
¼ pound butter, cut into cubes and kept cold
1 egg
⅓ cup milk

FILLING
1½ pounds each, blueberries, raspberries
    and blackberries
2 tablespoons water
1½ tablespoons sugar
1½ tablespoons cornstarch
1 tablespoon lemon juice

Preheat oven to 350°.
    Crumble together the flour, baking powder, sugar and butter until they have the texture of coarse cornmeal. Blend in egg and milk, mix and form into a ball.
    Roll dough on a floured surface to a ⅛" thickness. Using a template that is the same size and shape as the dish or dishes you are going to bake the cobbler in (these can be ⅔ cup individual dishes or a larger pyrex baking dish), cut the dough and chill it while you prepare the berries.
    Combine all ingredients for the filling in a saucepan and bring to a boil, stirring frequently. When the mixture is thick and syrupy, remove from the heat.

Spoon the mixture into baking dishes. Cover loosely with the crust and bake for 15 minutes, until the crust is lightly browned and the berry filling is bubbling out around the edges.
    Allow to cool a bit before serving.

Approximate preparation time: 1 hour.

FRESH BERRIES WITH CRÈME ANGLAISE

Oregon's Willamette Valley is justly renowned for its raspberries, its blueberries and the variety of its blackberries. Fresh berries are an ideal conclusion to any meal. Here's a light custard sauce used in our restaurants to complement the natural flavors of these summer beauties.

Makes about 2½ cups of sauce.

2½ cups milk
6 egg yolks
¼ cup sugar

Scald the milk and let it cool.
    Mix yolks and sugar with a wire whisk or electric mixer on *low* speed until thick and pale. Mixing constantly, slowly add the milk.
    Transfer mixture to a heavy saucepan or double boiler and cook, stirring constantly. Do not let it boil.
    When the custard is thick enough to coat the spoon, remove immediately from the heat to cool. (You can speed the cooling process by placing the saucepan in which the custard was cooked in a larger pan or bowl holding ice water.)
    Stir the mixture frequently as it cools to ensure a smooth texture.

Approximate preparation time: 15 minutes.

◀ *Three-Berry Cobbler*

MARSALA CUSTARD WITH BROWN SUGAR GLAZE

Recipes like this one make the modest investment in deep au gratin or custard dishes worthwhile. These dishes are extremely versatile and ensure the proper cooking of desserts and entrees alike. This custard, with the addition of the Marsala wine, is deliciously rich yet remarkably light.

Makes 6 portions, ⅔ cup each.

3 eggs
½ cup sugar
⅓ cup Marsala wine
3 cups cream
2 tablespoons brown sugar

Preheat oven to 300°.
　　Combine eggs, sugar, Marsala and cream and blend thoroughly but do *not* whip, as the frothy mixture produced by whipping disrupts the creamy texture of custard.
　　Pour the mixture into 6 custard dishes, ⅔" deep. If you don't have custard dishes, the custard can be baked in a large pyrex dish, as long as the depth of the custard is no more than 1".
　　Place custard dishes in a large roasting pan and pour water around them to ½ the height of the dishes.
　　Place roasting pan in oven and bake for 1 hour, until a toothpick stuck in the custard comes out clean and dry.
　　Remove custard and chill.
　　When you are ready to serve, preheat the oven broiler. Sift brown sugar over the surface of the custards in a very light coating. (Too much sugar or uneven lumps result in poor browning during the final step.)
　　Place custards about 2" below the broiler coils and brown the sugar until it is dark and bubbly. The sugar should be very brown but not quite burnt.

Approximate preparation time: 5 minutes preparation, 1 hour bake; 1 to 2 hours chill; 2 minutes under the broiler at serving time.

CHOCOLATE TRUFFLE CAKE SUNDAE

Okay, we admit it. We just couldn't give up the recipe for Jake's Famous Chocolate Truffle Cake. At least, not yet. So we offer you a couple of ways to embellish the store-bought version available in specialty grocery stores. Kids and adults alike are fans of sundaes and ice cream sandwiches. Here are the deluxe models.

Makes 4 sundaes.

1 Jake's Chocolate Truffle Cake, 16 ounces
Your favorite ice cream
Chocolate Fudge Sauce, heated
Walnuts, coarsely chopped for garnish
Raspberries for garnish
Whipped cream

Freeze truffle cake for 1 to 2 hours. This will make it easier to cut. (It will not freeze rock hard, so you will be able to cut it straight from the freezer. Cutting is also easier if you use a knife dipped in hot water between cuts.)
　　Trim the rounded edges of the cake to form a square. (These trimmed pieces, diced into small bits, can be kept almost indefinitely in zip-lock bags in your freezer and crumbled over or blended into ice cream for a great treat.) Once you've formed the square, quarter it into 4 smaller squares.
　　Place each of the cake squares on a dessert plate, top with the ice cream and pour on the warm fudge sauce. Sprinkle with nuts and berries, then finish with a dollop of whipped cream. Then kiss your waistline goodbye!

Approximate preparation time: 10 minutes.

◀ *Chocolate Truffle Cake Sundae*

CHOCOLATE TRUFFLE CAKE ICE CREAM SANDWICH

Makes 4 ice cream sandwiches.

1 Jake's Famous Chocolate Truffle Cake, 16 ounces
Your favorite ice cream

Trim the rounded edges of the cake to form a square. Then divide into 4 squares. Turn the squares on their edges and split them in ½.

Place 1 square of ice cream the same size as the cake on each of your divided cake squares. Set the remaining ½ square of cake on top and follow suit for each sandwich.

Refreeze the sandwiches until the ice cream is very firm, at least 1 hour.

Prepare for sticky fingers.

Approximate preparation time: 10 minutes.

DEEP-DISH APPLE PIE

The old-fashioned deep-dish apple pie served at McCormick & Schmick's in Portland is something to behold. Four inches deep and packed with apples, it's a pie lover's pie. If you want the real thing, purchase a deep, straight-sided, pie tin with a removable bottom and prepare to bake a beauty!

Makes 1 pie, 9" x 4".

CRUST
2 cups flour
4 tablespoons sugar
½ teaspoon salt
10 tablespoons butter, cold and cut into small cubes
3 to 4 tablespoons water
1 egg yolk

FILLING
16 cups sliced apples, about 14 to 16 large
    Granny Smith's or Newtons
1 tablespoon lemon juice
1 tablespoon cinnamon
6 tablespoons flour
1⅓ cups sugar
¼ cup water

STREUSEL TOPPING
1 cup flour
1 cup dark brown sugar
6 tablespoons butter or margarine

Remove all but the lower rack of your oven and preheat oven to 300°.

Prepare the crust by combining the flour, sugar and salt and working in the butter until the mixture resembles coarse cornmeal. Add the water and egg yolk and combine just enough to form a roll. Wrap in plastic and refrigerate for at least 1 hour.

The filling is prepared by combining the sliced apples with the remaining ingredients and blending thoroughly. Make sure all the apples are well coated.

Roll the pie dough out to about 18" diameter for the deep dish tin, line the tin with the dough, and flute the edge.

Add apple mixture so that it mounds well above the top of the shell, at least 2" or 3" in the center.

Combine the streusel ingredients and sprinkle liberally over the entire surface of the apples. There should be a pretty good coating of streusel.

Bake at 300° for 2½ to 3 hours, until well browned.

Remove the pie, allow to cool for 1 to 2 hours, then carefully and gently press the apples down into the pie until they are just about level with the crust. Refrigerate overnight to allow the pie to set. This procedure will firm the texture of the filling.

Remove the pie from the tin. (This is the reason you need a removable bottom—trying to cut this pie out of a tin does not work.) When you are ready to serve, reheat the pie and serve with a scoop of vanilla ice cream.

Approximate preparation time: 1 hour preparation; 3 hours baking; 2 hours cooling; overnight to chill.

CRANBERRY-PEAR CRISP

The Pacific Northwest is a major grower of cranberries. Oddly enough, fresh or frozen whole berries are hard to come by most of the year.

Makes 6 portions, ⅔ cup each.

TOPPING
¼ cup chopped and toasted pecans, walnuts or hazelnuts
⅔ cup oatmeal
¾ cup flour
½ cup brown sugar
2 teaspoons cinnamon
¼ pound margarine, cut into cubes
2 tablespoons water

FILLING
1 can whole cranberry sauce, 16-ounces
4 cups peeled, sliced fresh pears (about 4 large Anjou
    or Comice)
1 tablespoon cinnamon
1 tablespoon lemon juice

Preheat oven to 350°.
    Combine all dry ingredients for the topping and blend. (If you use hazelnuts, be sure to peel after roasting.)
    Crumble in the margarine cubes, combining and blending the mixture thoroughly. Add water to soften the mixture slightly and reserve.
    Place cranberry sauce in a large bowl and break it up with a spoon to loosen the gel. Don't overwork it or you will crush the whole berries. Add the pears, cinnamon and lemon juice and toss to combine.
    Transfer the mixture to a saucepan and cook over medium heat, stirring frequently until the pears soften. This takes just 3 to 4 minutes.
    Spoon mixture into individual serving dishes or a large pyrex dish, cover with topping and bake for 15 minutes, until the mixture is bubbly and the topping has browned.

Approximate preparation time: 45 minutes.

CHOCOLATE HAZELNUT PIE

This is the Pacific Northwest's answer to Southern-style pecan pie. A flaky crust, a gooey center and a layer of toasted hazelnuts and chocolate chips. It's been a standard on the dessert tray at the Harborside Restaurant in Portland since we opened. Toss out the diet and pass the unsweetened whipped cream.

Makes 1 pie, 9" in diameter

1 pie crust (See recipe, page 110.)
1 cup sugar
1⅓ cups dark corn syrup
7 tablespoons butter, cubed
6 eggs
½ tablespoon vanilla
1½ cups toasted, peeled and very coarsely chopped
    or halved hazelnuts
⅔ cup semi-sweet chocolate chips

Preheat oven to 300°.
    Prepare and roll out the pie crust and fit it into a 9" pie pan. Chill or freeze the shell until you are ready to fill.
    Combine sugar and syrup in a saucepan and bring to a boil, stirring constantly over medium heat. Cook at a boil for 2 minutes. Remove and cool for 10 to 15 minutes.
    Melt 1½ tablespoons of the butter in another saucepan and allow to brown slightly. Remove and cool.
    Beat the eggs. When the sugar mixture has cooled, add it to the eggs slowly, stirring constantly. Add the brown butter, the remaining cubed butter and the vanilla and stir until butter has melted and the mixture is well blended.
    Spread nuts and chocolate chips evenly over the bottom of the pie crust and pour in the egg-sugar-butter mixture.
    Bake for 1 hour to 1 hour and 15 minutes, until the filling has puffed up 1 to 1½ inches and is firm to the touch.
    Allow to cool thoroughly before cutting. (The filling will settle during cooling.)

Approximate preparation time: 2 hours.

LELAND'S
Salmon
Steak
/4.33LB

LELAND'S
Salmon
Fillet
7.99LB

LELAND'S
DUNGENESS
CRABS
2.99LB

LELAND'S
PACIFIC
OYSTERS
2.99LB

LELAND'S
OREGON MUSSELS
1.99LB

Basics

There is nothing more basic to the preparation of a fine meal than the selection, care and handling of the raw ingredients. In this chapter we give you a few guidelines to assist you in choosing seafood of the finest quality.

We have also included recipes that will serve you well in a variety of situations. These are the foundation sauces upon which our chefs rely. Many are traditional, but some offer a more contemporary approach and encourage your experimentation.

Finally, there are several ideas for side dishes to accompany the entrees. As you will see, we suggest simple, light preparations that allow the seafood to shine at center stage. It also helps that these side dishes are easily prepared, allowing more freedom to address the other details of your meal.

◄ *Basic to all our recipes is the finest, freshest seafood.*

Trying to cover, species by species, all of the factors that determine the quality of a piece of fish would require the page allotment of this entire book. However, some general rules apply to all fish.

When buying whole fish, look for bright, clear eyes, glistening skin, with most of the scales intact, and firm flesh. When buying filets, make sure that the flesh is bright and richly colored, moist and free from bruises, blood marks or separations. Again, the flesh should be firm and never mushy to the touch. As for smell, a piece of fresh fish smells fresh, never "fishy".

Salmon filets should be deep red; fresh tuna should be almost purple and bright, never opaque; bottom fish like sole and cod should be white, bright and moist. Halibut should be almost translucent, never chalky.

Get to know your fish merchant. Ask questions. Touch and feel the fish. Make sure you are getting what you need.

Once you get the fish home, take special care of it. First of all, you should try to use the fish soon, preferably that same day. If you must store the fish, wrap it well or seal it in an airtight plastic container and place it in the coldest part of your refrigerator. Change the wrappers or container at least every day.

Shellfish like clams, oysters and mussels should be scrubbed under cold running water, placed in a shallow container, covered with a damp cloth and, like all seafood, stored in the coldest part of your refrigerator. If any of the shellfish open before you use them, tap them with your fingers. If they respond by closing, they are fine; if not, discard them.

If you cut portions from large filets or loins, measure 1" to 1¼" thickness as a guideline or weigh them at 6 to 8 ounces.

When you cook, degree of doneness obviously depends on your preference. Our recommendation is that you cook fish such as salmon, swordfish, mahi mahi, sturgeon and ono to a stage best described as medium to medium rare. This is just barely cooked and still pink in the center. For fresh tuna, rare is preferred by some and fully cooked by others. For us, it depends on the recipe, but medium rare is the norm. Fish such as sole, cod and rockfish need to be cooked through, but just barely so that they are flaky, yet still moist.

We emphasize that what you want to avoid at all costs is overcooking. Texture, flavor and succulence are lost and what is left is unpalatable.

On pages 118 and 119, you may refer to the availability calendar for most Pacific Northwest seafood species. Use this guide and three basic rules: buy in season, buy fresh and buy quality.

BEURRE BLANC SAUCE

Makes about 1 cup.

6 ounces white wine
3 ounces white wine vinegar
3 whole black peppercorns
1 shallot, cut into quarters
1 cup heavy cream
6 ounces cold, unsalted butter, cut into pieces
3 ounces cold butter, cut into pieces

Combine wine, vinegar, peppercorns and shallot in a noncorrosive saucepan (stainless steel, teflon, calphalon).

Reduce until the mixture is just 1 to 2 tablespoons and has the consistency of syrup.

Add cream and reduce again until mixture is 3 to 4 tablespoons and very syrupy. Remove pan from heat!

Add butters, about 2 ounces at a time, stirring constantly and allowing each addition to melt in before adding more. (If mixture cools too much, butter will not melt completely and you'll have to reheat slightly.)

Strain and hold warm on a stove-top trivet or in a double-boiler over very low heat until you are ready to use it.

NOTE: This sauce may be flavored with orange, lemon, spices, herbs, berry or fruit concentrates. These may be added at the end or during the reduction of the cream.

COMPOUND BUTTERS

Add to 1 pound butter:

FLAVORING OPTIONS:
- ▶ ½ cup roasted red peppers and 4 tablespoons minced shallots
- ▶ 4 tablespoons dijon mustard, 4 tablespoons chopped fresh basil or 4 teaspoons dry basil, 2 tablespoons minced shallots
- ▶ 4 tablespoons chopped cilantro, 1 tablespoon cumin, 4 tablespoons chopped green chilies
- ▶ ½ cup toasted, peeled and chopped hazelnuts and 4 tablespoons lemon zest
- ▶ ½ cup roasted garlic puree and 4 tablespoons chopped parsley
- ▶ 4 tablespoons pureed fresh ginger and 4 tablespoons lemon zest

Soften the butter in a blender or food processor to room temperature. Add the specified flavorings and puree until fully blended.

Place butter on a 12" piece of plastic wrap or waxed paper. Arrange butter in a 6" to 8" long by 1" to 1½" wide log. Roll the paper to form a cylinder of butter and twist the ends. It will look like a very long, very fat piece of saltwater taffy.

Freeze butter at least 2 hours until solid.

Alternately, you can place the blended butter in a pastry bag fitted with a large star tip and pipe rosettes of butter onto a cookie sheet. Freeze the rosettes. Once they are frozen, they can be removed from the sheet and kept in a sealed container or freezer bag.

MIGNONETTE SAUCE

Makes 4 tablespoons.

¼ cup red wine vinegar
2 teaspoons finely chopped shallots
½ teaspoon freshly ground pepper

Combine the vinegar, shallots and pepper and serve at room temperature.

TARTAR SAUCE

Makes approximately 3 cups.

⅓ cup finely minced celery
⅓ cup finely minced onion
2 cups mayonnaise, homemade or commercial
2 tablespoons lemon juice
1 teaspoon Worcestershire sauce
Pinch salt
Pinch dry mustard
Pinch pepper
2 tablespoons dill pickle relish

Combine all ingredients and mix well.

HOLLANDAISE SAUCE

Makes about 1½ cups.

½ pound unsalted butter, melted and warm, but not hot
3 egg yolks
1 tablespoon water
1 tablespoon lemon juice
Pinch salt

Melt the butter and reserve. Combine the egg yolks and water in the top of a double boiler over hot, but not boiling water, and stir briskly with a wire whisk until the mixture is light and fluffy and the consistency of light mayonnaise.

Remove the top of the double boiler from the heat and slowly add the butter in a thin stream, while continuing to whip the mixture.

Season the mixture with the lemon juice and salt to taste.

BÉARNAISE SAUCE

Makes about 1½ cups.

¼ cup tarragon vinegar
3 springs fresh tarragon (or 1 teaspoon dried)
3 sprigs fresh chervil (or 1 teaspoon dried)
2 shallots, finely chopped

Combine the vinegar, herbs and shallots over medium heat and reduce to approximately 1 tablespoon of thick paste. Allow to cool slightly. Add paste to Hollandaise in place of lemon juice.

JALAPEÑO HOLLANDAISE

Makes about 1½ cups.

Proceed as for Hollandaise, but add one very finely minced jalapeño pepper to the egg and water mixture cooking in the double boiler.

1000 ISLAND DRESSING

Makes approximately 4 cups.

½ cup finely diced celery
½ cup finely diced onion
2 cups mayonnaise, homemade or commercial
1 tablespoon Worcestershire sauce
1 tablespoon prepared horseradish
¾ cup chili sauce
2 tablespoons lemon juice
2 tablespoons dill pickle relish
Pinch salt
Pinch pepper

Combine all ingredients and mix well.

DILL SAUCE

Makes 2 cups.

1 cup sour cream
½ cup mayonnaise
¼ cup freshly chopped dill (or 2 tablespoons dried)
2 tablespoons milk or cream
1 tablespoon lemon juice
Salt and white pepper to taste

Combine all ingredients and blend thoroughly.

FRESH SALSA

Fresh salsas, once exclusively associated with Mexican cuisine, are the ideal accompaniments for many varieties of grilled seafood. All of the chefs in our company have lent their creativity to developing these light and flavorful salsas. Once you try the basic recipe and a couple of variations, you just might be inspired to create some salsas of your own.

Makes approximately 2½ cups.

1 cup peeled, seeded and chopped tomatoes
⅓ cup diced red onions.
½ cup diced, multi-colored peppers (red, green, yellow)
2 tablespoons chopped cilantro
½ tablespoon cumin
1 teaspoon chili powder
1 teaspoon minced garlic
¼ cup olive oil
1 tablespoon lime juice
Minced jalapeño pepper, to taste (1 for medium,
     2 for hot, 3 for very hot)
1 teaspoon salt
¼ cup commercial salsa (optional) if you like your salsa
     to have a looser consistency

Combine all ingredients and blend well.

NOTE: Commercial salsa, with more liquid in the mix, has a less chunky (but also less fresh) look. It all depends on your preference, as does the heat level of your salsa.

PAPAYA-CHILI SALSA

Makes approximately 1½ cups.

1 papaya, firm but ripe, peeled, seeded and diced
    into ¼" chunks
1 small jalapeño, seeded and minced
1 tablespoon chopped mint
1 tablespoon finely diced red onion
1 teaspoon cumin
Pinch chili powder
2 tablespoons rice wine vinegar
1 tablespoon olive oil

Combine all ingredients and mix thoroughly.

MINTED AVOCADO SALSA

Makes approximately 1½ cups.

1 avocado, firm but ripe, peeled, pitted and diced
    into ¼" chunks
1 small tomato, peeled, seeded and diced
3 tablespoons chopped mint
6 tablespoons olive oil
4 tablespoons rice wine vinegar
1 teaspoon salt
1 teaspoon cumin
1 teaspoon chili powder

Combine all ingredients and mix thoroughly.

CAJUN BLACKENING SPICE

Makes 1 cup.

4 tablespoons paprika
1½ tablespoons salt
1½ tablespoons onion powder
1½ tablespoons garlic powder
1 tablespoon white pepper
1 tablespoon black pepper
1½ tablespoons cayenne pepper
2 tablespoons thyme
2 tablespoons oregano

Combine and mix thoroughly. Store in air tight container.

NOTE: A Southwestern variation on this mixture is made by substituting cumin for paprika, chili powder for cayenne and 4 tablespoons cilantro for thyme and oregano.

COCKTAIL SAUCE

Makes approximately 2 cups.

1 cup commercial chili sauce
½ cup catsup
2 tablespoons horseradish
1 teaspoon lemon juice
1 teaspoon Worcestershire sauce
½ teaspoon dry mustard
½ teaspoon black pepper
1 teaspoon Tabasco
¼ teaspoon salt

Combine all ingredients and mix well.

WARM BACON DRESSING

Makes about 2 cups.

½ pound bacon, chopped fine
½ tablespoon basil
1 teaspoon marjoram
½ teaspoon salt
¼ teaspoon black pepper
½ cup vinegar
½ tablespoon lemon juice
1 small garlic clove, minced
2 tablespoons sugar

Over low heat, cook bacon until brown and crisp. Reserve the bacon grease.
    Combine all ingredients and mix.
    Serve warm.

NOTE: This dressing may be refrigerated and reheated.

PIE CRUST

Makes 1 deep dish pie crust.

½ pound unsalted butter, very cold, cut into small pieces
2 cups flour
2 teaspoons sugar
1 teaspoon salt
3 to 4 tablespoons cold water

Combine the butter, flour, sugar and salt and blend either lightly by hand or in a food processor until the mixture resembles coarse cornmeal.
    Add the water, a little at a time, and blend until the dough forms a solid ball. If you are using a food processor, this step should take less than one minute.
    Knead the dough briefly and gently on a floured surface to form a firm dough. Refrigerate the pastry for at least one hour before rolling out.

VEGETABLES and ACCOMPANIMENTS

The following fresh vegetable and starch dishes are used by many of our chefs. They are relatively simple, straightforward, traditional accompaniments that complement our seafood entrees perfectly. The key is to use only the freshest, finest produce you can find.

ASPARAGUS with SAFFRON AIOLI

Serves 4.

1½ pounds asparagus
½ teaspoon saffron
1 tablespoon very hot water
2 egg yolks
1 garlic clove, peeled and crushed
1 cup olive oil
1 teaspoon lemon juice

If the asparagus is large, peel the stalks. However, we prefer very thin, young asparagus, which we do not peel. Blanch the asparagus in boiling water until just barely tender. Plunge into very cold water to halt cooking and seal color. Drain and reserve.
    Steep the saffron in hot water for 5 minutes to draw out its flavor and color. Place the saffron, water, egg yolks and garlic in the bowl of a food processor or blender and blend for 1 minute. With the motor still running, very slowly add the oil as you would in the preparation of mayonnaise. When all the oil has been incorporated, add the lemon juice.
    You may serve the asparagus chilled or heated, with the aioli poured over or served to the side.

GREEN BEANS WITH ROASTED RED PEPPER BUTTER

Serves 4.

1 pound young, thin green beans, trimmed
3 tablespoons roasted red pepper butter
    (See recipe, page 107.)
Salt and pepper to taste.

Blanch the beans in boiling water. If the beans are very fine and thin, this should take no more than 3 or 4 minutes. They should be just barely cooked through. Drain the beans and plunge them into very cold water. This halts the cooking and ensures a bright green color. Drain and reserve.

When you are ready to serve, heat the beans in butter over medium-high heat and sprinkle with salt and pepper.

CARROTS AND SNOWPEAS IN GINGER BUTTER

Serves 4.

¾ pound snowpeas, trimmed
½ pound carrots, peeled and cut into 2" julienne
2 tablespoons butter
2 tablespoons sherry
½ tablespoon finely chopped fresh ginger
½ tablespoon lemon juice

Blanch the snowpeas and carrots separately in boiling water for 1 to 2 minutes. Plunge into cold water to halt the cooking process and seal colors.

Melt the butter over medium heat and add the sherry, ginger and lemon juice. Cook for 1 minute.

Add the carrots to the pan and continue cooking for 1 more minute. Then add the snowpeas and complete the cooking for 1 to 2 final minutes.

SAUTÉED SPINACH WITH OIL AND VINEGAR

Serves 4.

2 pounds spinach, coarse stems removed, washed
    and drained
2 tablespoons butter
¼ thinly sliced yellow onion (optional)
Salt and freshly ground pepper to taste
Extra virgin olive oil
Balsamic vinegar

Cook the spinach in boiling water for 1 to 2 minutes. Drain and plunge the spinach into very cold water to arrest cooking and seal color.

Remove the spinach and squeeze it to extract as much water as is possible. Reheat the spinach by sautéing it over medium heat in butter. If you wish to add the onions, start them in the pan first. When they begin to soften, add the spinach for 2 to 3 minutes, to reheat.

Season with salt and freshly ground pepper and serve the oil and vinegar from cruets at your table.

STEAMED RED POTATOES IN PARSLEY BUTTER

Serves 4.

16-20 new red potatoes, the smaller the better
3 tablespoons butter
3 tablespoons chopped parsley
Salt and pepper to taste

If the potatoes you use are very small, they can be cooked whole. If they are golf ball size or larger, they should be halved.
Cook the potatoes in salted water to cover until they are tender.
Melt the butter in a saucepan and add the parsley and cooked potatoes. Season with salt and pepper.

NOTE: There's nothing simpler to prepare than parsleyed potatoes. The bonus is that they go well with almost any grilled or broiled seafood.

RICE PILAF

Serves 4.

1 cup raw white rice
3 tablespoons butter
1 tablespoon minced onion
1 tablespoon minced celery
1 tablespoon minced carrot
¼ teaspoon dried thyme or dill
¼ teaspoon black pepper
3 cups good quality, strong chicken stock or bouillon

Preheat the oven to 350°.
Heat the butter over medium flame and sauté the vegetables for 1 to 2 minutes.
Add the rice and seasonings and continue sautéing for an additional 2 to 3 minutes. Add the stock and stir to blend.
Transfer the rice mixture to a baking dish and bake covered until the rice has absorbed all the liquid, approximately 45 minutes.

SCALLOPED POTATOES

Serves 4 to 6.

2 pounds medium-sized, waxy potatoes, red or
    yellow varieties
1 garlic clove, peeled
1½ cups milk
1 egg yolk
1 tablespoon flour
¼ teaspoon salt
¼ teaspoon pepper
4 tablespoons butter

Preheat the oven to 350°.
Peel and thinly slice the potatoes.
Combine the remaining ingredients, except the butter, and blend in a food processor or blender.
Layer the potato slices in a medium-size baking dish, overlapping them slightly. Pour the milk mixture over the potatoes and dot with butter.
Bake for 45 minutes, until the potatoes are tender and the top of the dish has browned.

NOTE: If you like cheese on your scalloped potatoes, scatter 1 cup of shredded cheddar or other mild cheese over the dish for the last 20 minutes of baking.

ACINI DE PEPE WITH TOMATO-PEPPER "DUXELLES"

Serves 4.

3 cups cooked acini (See NOTE.)
3 tablespoons olive oil
2 tablespoons minced onion
4 tablespoons minced green pepper
4 tablespoons finely chopped, peeled and seeded tomato
1 tablespoon chopped parsley
½ tablespoon chopped garlic
¼ teaspoon salt
¼ teaspoon pepper

Cook the acini, following package directions.

Sauté the onions and peppers in the olive oil for 1 to 2 minutes over medium heat.

Add the tomato, parsley and garlic and continue cooking until the tomato liquid has evaporated. Season.

Add the cooked acini to the pan and toss to mix and heat thoroughly.

Optionally, the tomato-pepper mixture can be used as a topping for the acini.

NOTE: Acini is a very small, round pasta. It is readily available in major grocery stores.

ORZO WITH WILD RICE IN HERB BUTTER

Serves 4.

2 cups cooked orzo (See NOTE.)
1 cup cooked wild rice (See NOTE.)
3 tablespoons butter
½ tablespoon chopped fresh basil (or ½ teaspoon dried)
½ tablespoon chopped fresh oregano
   (or ½ teaspoon dried)
½ tablespoon chopped fresh thyme
   (or ½ teaspoon dried)
1 tablespoon chopped shallots
½ teaspoon salt
½ teaspoon pepper

Cook the orzo and wild rice according to package instructions.

Melt the butter over medium heat and add the herbs, shallots, salt and pepper and cook for 1 minute. Add the orzo and rice and toss to blend and heat thoroughly.

NOTE: Orzo is a small, rice-shaped pasta also called Rosa marina. Both orzo and wild rice are available in major grocery stores.

INDEX

Acknowledgments

We would like to thank the following people for their gracious assistance and support throughout the development of this book: Sara Perry, Linda Dixon, Bette Sinclair, Katharine McCanna, Carl Greve Jewelers with special thanks to Kathleen Taggart, Zell Bros. Jewelers, Kitchen Kaboodle, Ann Sack's Tile—especially Casey Sax and Leland's Meat and Seafood Market.

McCormick & Schmick Management Group
720 S.W. Washington, Suite 550
Portland, OR 97205
(503) 226-3440

The McCormick & Schmick retail division offers fresh Northwest seafood delivered directly to you via door-to-door express service.
Monday-Friday, 8am-5pm PST, 1-800-777-7179.

PORTLAND

Jake's Famous Crawfish
401 S.W. Twelfth Street
(503) 226-1419

Jake's Backstage
1111 S.W. Broadway
(503) 220-1888

McCormick & Schmick's
235 S.W. First Avenue
(503) 224-7522

Jake's Catering
1111 S.W. Broadway
(503) 220-1888

McCormick & Schmick's
Harborside Restaurant
& Pilsner Room
0309 S.W. Montgomery
(503) 220-1865

McCormick's Fish House
9945 S.W. Bvtn-Hlsdl Hwy.
(503) 643-1322

SEATTLE

McCormick's Fish House
722 Fourth Avenue
(206) 682-3900

McCormick & Schmick's
1103 First Avenue
(206) 623-5500

DENVER

McCormick's Fish House
1659 Wazee
(303) 825-1107

IRVINE

McCormick & Schmick's
2000 Main Street
(714) 756-0505

LOS ANGELES

McCormick & Schmick's
633 West Fifth Street
4th Floor
(213) 629-1929

SAN FRANCISCO

McCormick & Kuleto's
900 North Point Street
(415) 929-1730

PASADENA

McCormick & Schmick's
111 N. Los Robles
(818) 405-0064

Seafood Availability Calendar

These seasons fluctuate slightly from year to year and availability is always subject to weather and fishing conditions. However, this list will provide you with guidelines for your Northwest seafood purchases.

JANUARY

Alaskan Winter Troll King Salmon
Oregon Dungeness Crab
Pacific Northwest Coastal Rockfish
Pacific Northwest Coastal Sole
Pacific Northwest Coastal True Cod and Ling Cod
Pacific Northwest Manila Clams

FEBRUARY

Alaskan Winter Troll King Salmon
Columbia River Spring Chinook Salmon
Columbia River Steelhead
Columbia River Sturgeon
Oregon Dungeness Crab
Pacific Northwest Coastal Rockfish
Pacific Northwest Coastal Sole
Pacific Northwest Coastal True Cod and Ling Cod
Pacific Northwest Manila Clams

MARCH

Alaskan Winter Troll King Salmon
Columbia River Spring Chinook Salmon
Columbia River Steelhead
Columbia River Sturgeon
Oregon Dungeness Crab
Pacific Northwest Coastal Rockfish
Pacific Northwest Coastal Sole
Pacific Northwest Coastal True Cod and Ling Cod
Pacific Northwest Manila Clams

APRIL

Alaskan Winter Troll King Salmon
Oregon Crawfish
Oregon Dungeness Crab
Pacific Northwest Bay Shrimp
Pacific Northwest Coastal Rockfish
Pacific Northwest Coastal Sole
Pacific Northwest Coastal True Cod and Ling Cod
Pacific Northwest Manila Clams

MAY

Oregon Crawfish
Oregon Dungeness Crab (supply becomes limited)
Oregon/Washington Troll King Salmon
Pacific Northwest Bay Shrimp
Pacific Northwest Coastal Rockfish
Pacific Northwest Coastal Sole
Pacific Northwest Coastal True Cod and Ling Cod
Pacific Northwest Halibut
Pacific Northwest Manila Clams
Pacific Northwest Razor Clams
Specialty King Salmon (Copper River)

JUNE

Alaskan Dungeness Crab
Oregon Crawfish
Oregon Dungeness Crab (supply becomes limited)
Oregon Troll Coho Salmon
Oregon/Washington Troll King Salmon
Pacific Northwest Bay Shrimp
Pacific Northwest Coastal Rockfish
Pacific Northwest Coastal Sole
Pacific Northwest Coastal True Cod and Ling Cod
Pacific Northwest Halibut
Pacific Northwest Manila Clams
Pacific Northwest Razor Clams
Specialty King Salmon (Copper and Kenai Rivers)